Frederick Warne, 1825-1901

THE HOUSE OF
⋆ WARNE ⋆

ONE HUNDRED YEARS OF PUBLISHING

TOLD BY
ARTHUR KING
AND
A. F. STUART

FREDERICK WARNE & CO LTD:
LONDON
FREDERICK WARNE & CO INC:
NEW YORK

TEXT PRINTED BY

Butler & Tanner Ltd, Frome and London

HALF-TONE PLATES PRINTED BY

Frederick Warne & Co Ltd, London

PAPER SUPPLIED BY

A. H. James & Co Ltd, London

HALF-TONE BLOCKS ENGRAVED BY

West End Engraving Co Ltd

COVER DESIGNED BY

Cécile Curtis

COVER PRINTED BY

Edmund Evans Ltd, London

COVER MATERIAL SUPPLIED BY

Thomas Goodall & Co Ltd, London

BINDING BRASSES ENGRAVED BY

T. Mackrell & Co, London

BLOCKED AND BOUND BY

The Newdigate Press Ltd, Dorking, Surrey

LIBRARY OF CONGRESS CATALOG CARD No. 65.27894

PRINTED IN GREAT BRITAIN

Contents

Preface

A reviewer once said (and being vain we kept a note of it):
"In our household we keep Beatrix Potter and Shakespeare on
the same shelf." The combination of names may strike one
as being rather startling at first, but there is a slightly more
subtle connection here than this reviewer had in mind. For
the centenary of Shakespeare's birth was celebrated in 1964—in
quadruplicate as befits his greatness—and following on three
hundred years behind, Frederick Warne & Company, Beatrix
Potter's publishers, celebrate theirs in this year of 1965, while
the lady herself is due for a similar honour in 1966. It is a
pleasure to know that we are in such good company.

There is, after all, a sense of occasion about a centenary. A
name, an institution or a business house which survives to see
out a hundred years has at least a certain toughness of fibre
about it and a will to live—something, one imagines, that
makes it tick. And so it is with publishers, who often seem at
times like the swan in Tennyson's poem, to have seen many a
summer. Quite a number of well-known names in the publishing world today were there a century ago: Routledge, Cassell,
Longman's, Chapman & Hall, Batsford, Macmillan, to name
a few, and some are obviously still in very good fettle. We our-
selves still have enough household names on our list—Beatrix
Potter, Leslie Brooke, Kate Greenaway, Dr Nuttall (Edward
Lear we might have included, but he is now common property)
—to keep us in business for the present, and a sufficient number
of up-and-coming authors and artists to form, with the Wayside and Woodland and Observer's series, a basis for the
future.

That the average reader develops an appreciation for Beatrix
Potter earlier in life than a concern for the prose of James
Joyce, for instance, we can only regard as our good fortune; one
must start somewhere, even though it may be to a particular
publisher's advantage.

Although no man can foretell the future, we are very proud
in the year of 1965 to be celebrating our first centenary, and

are still in business, receiving orders and fulfilling them, reading books, printing books, binding books, selling books and sometimes, being human, probably cursing books occasionally. Yet in spite of the possible frustration (and what is more complicated a piece of merchandise than a book?) there is after all nothing like a good book and one must have been very unlucky in life not to have obtained tremendous pleasure at some time or other from a book's companionship.

We should like at this point to pay tribute to many of our old business friends who have helped us so consistently at all times over the past years, the paper makers and agents, printers and bookbinders, who have by their excellent work and service, enabled us to keep our place in the ever-changing world of publishing. Neither must we forget that vast host of booksellers all over the globe who have loyally ordered and stocked our publications. May we also finally pay tribute to the many scores of authors and artists whose original inspiration, even though it sometimes may have only survived one fifteen-hundred printing run, made our business possible and our centenary a reality.

*From "The Tale of Johnny Town-
Mouse" by Beatrix Potter*

CHAPTER I

Origins

The first of the Warnes to enter the book trade was William Henry, who as a youth of fifteen joined the bookselling business of George Routledge when it started in September 1836 at 11 Ryders Court, Leicester Square, in London's West End, then mainly a residential district. This was an inauspicious beginning, but events took a more definite turn in the following year in 1837 when George Routledge married William's sister Marie Elizabeth. The business evidently prospered, as in 1843 Routledge added publishing to his bookselling business and in 1848 he took his young brother-in-law into partnership, adding a further partner to the business in 1851 when the firm became Routledge & Company. This later partner was William's younger brother Frederick Warne, who was already working with them in the business.

These brothers were two of the twelve children of Edmund Warne, a builder, and of his wife Matilda, a daughter of a Mr R. A. Stannard. Frederick, who was later to found the business which bears his name, was born as their sixth and youngest son on the 13th October 1825 in the City of Westminster and was privately educated in nearby Soho.

The business continued until 1858, when Robert Warne Routledge, son of George, joined the partnership and the firm's name was again changed, this time to Routledge, Warne & Routledge. A year later, in 1859, William Henry, the elder of the two Warne brothers, died at the early age of thirty-eight. Frederick however still continued with the firm for a few more years and there was no doubt that his flair and industry contributed much to the success of Routledge, Warne & Routledge. When he finally left the Company it was already a well-established and renowned business. In 1865

1

his partnership with the Routledges was dissolved by mutual consent, and both parties were to go their separate ways in the book trade, the one continuing as George Routledge & Sons and the other as Frederick Warne & Company, whose centenary this volume commemorates.

A London street of the period,
drawing by Moira Hoddell

Plate 2

From *Marigold Garden* by Kate Greenaway

CHAPTER 2

Early Days, 1865-1894

The firm of Frederick Warne & Company started business on
1st July 1865, with offices at 15 Bedford Street, Covent Garden,
where it has, with the subsequent addition of the Bedford
Court premises, continued its activities to the present day.

The site is not without its associations, as in the early seven-
teenth century Chief Justice Sir Thomas Richardson is reputed
to have lived in a house there, and later the residence was
occupied by a bookseller named Lilly. In the eighteenth century Dr Johnson sometimes dined at Thomas Sheridan's house
a door or two away, and from the window his friend would
watch the Doctor's approach along Henrietta Street, touching
all the street posts as he passed them. Bedford Court's claim to
fame is that in 1740 White's Coffee House was located there, as
was also a bookseller named William Sare, with a shop-sign
of the "Caesar's Head".

Venturing a little further afield, Warne's Bedford Street
premises are only a few short yards from that street's conjunction with Chandos Place, almost at the corner of which the
poor boy Charles Dickens pasted labels on pots in a blacking
warehouse, in conditions of shame he was to recall with such
sorrow in later life. By 1865 he was the greatest novelist of the
day, however, and his publishers, Chapman & Hall, were for
many years in nearby Henrietta Street.

Today the area boasts a strange mixture of fruit and publishing and the offices of some local publishers are placed cheek
by jowl with perhaps a wholesale fruit warehouse, books being
unloaded at one door while a consignment of apples arrives at
the next.

When Frederick Warne's partnership with the Routledges
was dissolved, the catalogue of Routledge, Warne & Routledge
was divided up so that the new house of Warne commenced
business with a substantial number of standard books.

In the first catalogue issued by Frederick Warne under the

date of 30th June 1865, appeared the following announcement:

"Routledge, Warne & Routledge—Expiration of Partnership.
Mr Frederick Warne takes this opportunity of announc-
ing to the Trade his complete secession from the above
well-known Publishing Firm, and his commencement of
business on his own account as General Publisher and
Commission Agent, under the style and title of Frederick
Warne and Company at 15 Bedford Street, Covent Garden,
where he requests all communications to be now addressed.

He also desires to express his personal thanks to all with
whom he has had business transactions during the term of his
late Partnership, and now solicits a renewal of the same for his
new Firm, assuring them that his most constant exertions
shall be given to maintain the friendly intercourse that he
has so long enjoyed."

Great moral support in the launching of the new firm came
from Frederick Warne's friend George Smith the second, of the
publishing house of Smith, Elder & Company, which was
founded in 1816 and was now in 1865 situated at 65 Cornhill,
London, and had published the works of Thackeray and the
Brontës among many others, and founded the *Cornhill Magazine.*

Also associated with the new venture from its beginnings
were Edward James Dodd, a colleague and friend from Routledges and Armand William Duret, who left the printing firm
of Daziel Brothers to join in with the others. Duret retired in
1879 and Dodd left the business in 1895.

Frederick Warne, who had started work at the age of fourteen and now at forty years of age had twenty-five years of
bookselling and publishing experience behind him, then pro-
ceeded to put this to good use with an abounding energy. The
production of new books was a very quick process in those
days so that the new firm was able to add very considerably to
its catalogue within a few months.

Perhaps one of the most outstanding series which had very
extensive sales in those early days and proved a great factor
in enlightening the reading public, which was then developing
with the gradual spread of education, was the Chandos Classics.

This series of ultimately 154 titles comprised all classes of literature and included nearly all the standard poets as well as the leading prose works within its range. The books were published at one shilling and sixpence in paper covers, and at two shillings in cased cloth. The total sales exceeded five million copies, the Shakespeare alone topping 340,000. The series can be looked upon as among the fore-runners of the well-known series of classics which are on the market at the present day.

Another famous publication from the very earliest days was Nuttall's *Standard Dictionary*, which Frederick Warne had inherited as part of his share of the old Routledge, Warne & Routledge catalogue. The book was originally published by the older company in 1863 and was first issued with the Warne imprint in January 1867. 668,000 copies were eventually sold and a revised edition issued in 1886 had sold nearly a million copies by 1911. The title is still very much with us in this centenary year and today the name Nuttall carries a goodwill which now extends to cover a whole range of books of an allied nature.

Perhaps a word or two at this point regarding the original Dr Peter Austin Nuttall would not be out of place. He was born at Ormskirk, Lancashire, and became a scholar at Ormskirk Grammar School. He later acquired a sound knowledge and love of Latin and Greek which distinguished much of his editorial work. His first book, a new edition of Stirling's *Satires of Juvenal*, was published in August 1825 by Thomas Ward of High Holborn, London, and later came a revised edition of Virgil's *Bucolics*.

In 1839 Dr Nuttall became a partner with a Mr C. F. Hodgson in a printing business at 1 Gough Square, Fleet Street, and his first major work to be issued by that firm was his *Classical Dictionary*. Later he edited Walker's *Pronouncing Dictionary*, a pocket edition of Samuel Johnson's *Dictionary*, Webster's *Pronouncing Dictionary* and Craig's *The Universal English Dictionary*. In 1863 Routledge, Warne & Routledge published the first edition of the *Standard Pronouncing Dictionary of the English Language* which bore his name. He died in December 1869 at the age of seventy-six.

THE

STANDARD

PRONOUNCING DICTIONARY

OF THE

ENGLISH LANGUAGE:

BASED ON THE LABOURS OF

WORCESTER,	GOODRICH,	CRAIG,
RICHARDSON,	JOHNSON,	OGILVIE,
WEBSTER,	WALKER,	TRENCH,

AND OTHER EMINENT LEXICOGRAPHERS:

COMPRISING MANY THOUSAND NEW WORDS
WHICH MODERN LITERATURE, SCIENCE, ART, AND FASHION HAVE CALLED
INTO EXISTENCE

A New Edition.

EDITED BY

P. AUSTIN NUTTALL, LL.D..

COMPILER OF NUMEROUS EDUCATIONAL WORKS

LONDON:

FREDERICK WARNE & Co.,

15, BEDFORD STREET, COVENT GARDEN.

1868.

An early title page

It is impossible to enumerate many of the hundreds of books published during the early years of the history of the firm, but mention might be made of a few of them. Among the authors and works Mr Warne included in his early catalogues were:

Miss Wetherell, author of *Ellen Montgomery's Book Shelf, The Wide, Wide World, Queechy* and others.
Montgomery's *Poems*.
Half Hours with the Best Authors, edited by Charles Knight.
British Rural Sports, by Stonehenge.
A Manual of Domestic Medicine and Surgery, by J. H. Walsh, F.R.C.S.
The Book of Nonsense, by Edward Lear.
Gay's Fables, with 126 illustrations.
Aesop's Fables.
King Arthur and the Knights of the Round Table.
The Everyday Book of Natural History, by James Cundall.

The principle by which the founder of the business selected all his publications can be explained in an announcement in the *Monthly List* for September 1865. This was with regard to a new edition of the *Arabian Nights' Entertainments* which was publicized as follows:

"Without the least destroying the imagery of any of the stories, or omitting any of the tales or incidents, the Editor has been able to expurgate entirely *the parts that parents consider objectionable for their children to read*, and also to explain in short notes the origin and peculiarities of most of the Oriental customs and habits."

It is evident from the fore-going that mid-Victorian families accepted an outward moral code which was laid down in a very decided black-and-white and which did not, as in our later days, fade off into an indeterminate grey.

With regard to Frederick Warne's own family life, he had married a Miss Louisa Jane Fruing, of Jersey, and they first lived in Doughty Street, near Gray's Inn. Frederick used to tell his family that he married on the profits of *Uncle Tom's Cabin*, the right to print which he bought from the U.S.A. They had

six children, the first of whom, Fred, died early in life in
Germany. Then came Edith, Harold, Fruing, Amelia (Milly)
and Norman, the three boys following into the business at the
end of their schooldays.

On leaving their Doughty Street home, the Warnes went to
live at 8 Bedford Square, one of Bloomsbury's most charming
squares, and even today, in 1965, a quiet Georgian oasis in a
district now, alas, scarred and built on beyond all recognition.
It was here that Frederick kept open house for his relatives,
friends and business acquaintances, and being himself of a
jovial turn of mind, was never more pleased than when seeing
his large dining-room table surrounded with people at the
family mid-day meal.

He was also very fond of a game of whist or cribbage, both
of which he taught his children and grandchildren early in
their lives. Although he was fond of taking long drives in a
carriage round the countryside, his main out-door recreation

A mid-Victorian dining-room,
drawing by Moira Hoddell

was fishing, and much of his leisure time was spent at Slapton Lea in Devon in search of pike, perch and roach. Later on, when his married daughter Edith lived at West Bay, Bridport, on the Dorset coast, he would take a small boat out to sea to catch mackerel.

As regards the Company's staff or their conditions during the very early days of the period under review, we unfortunately at this stage have very scanty knowledge, but within the memory of the oldest serving members still with us today is acquaintance with older men who had served the firm during the 1880's and 1890's when they in turn were young. That the conditions were possibly hard, hours long, and the wages relatively poor by today's standards is no doubt the case and would be typical of the period, but Warne's have from the earliest days had a hard core of loyal staff so there must have been compensations.

If we may be permitted one or two anecdotes at this point in our story, we can recall hearing from Mr "Teddy" Barnard (later Town traveller) how as a youth in the 1880's he had fought shy of acquiring a top hat, much to the annoyance of Frederick Warne who liked to see his staff suitably attired. Finally young Barnard was called into the "old man's" office one day and saw before him on the desk a row of top hats of varying styles and sizes. He was promptly ordered to try them on for size, choose the one that fitted and consider it thenceforward as part of his outdoor equipment.

Another story that can be told regarding the conventional Victorian attitude to dress, concerns Frederick Warne and his young son Norman. The latter, who was going out for a country ramble one week-end, turned up on a Saturday morning dressed for the part. Frederick, meeting him by chance at the door, looked at him in amazement and promptly sent him back to Bedford Square to change into the usual black coat and waistcoat and striped trousers of the period.

Frederick Warne also had a habit of calling all the members of his junior staff "Mister", and incidentally at Bedford Square called all his male servants "John" and the female ones "Mary".

"Hi, Mister," he once called to a new boy, "I want you to

From "*Nonsense Omnibus*"
by *Edward Lear*

take this letter to my house in Bedford Square. Here's half a crown for a cab and half a crown for your dinner. Now make haste!"

The new boy in question, by name Harry Messenger and later the firm's Binding Manager, pocketed the five shillings, equal to a week's wages for a beginner in those days, and ran both ways, probably ultimately spending sevenpence on a cut from the joint and two veg. and sweet, which even as late as 1914 could be had for sevenpence at what might be called a good pull-up for carmen. With Covent Garden Market so near to the firm's premises, there must always have been cafés and eating-houses where plain fare at modest prices was customary.

During the whole of this period the publication of healthy literature at popular prices continued to be the steady aim of the partners. Besides the greater names of Kate Greenaway, Randolph Caldecott and Edward Lear, whose works for children the firm consistently sold in large numbers over many years, were others whose books were included as titles in various series of vast proportions, notable examples of which were the Crown Library at two shillings, containing upwards of 60 volumes; Warne's Star Series, published at one shilling and

sixpence and two shillings, with some 130 volumes, and the
Notable Novels at sixpence, containing over 150 volumes.

During the 1880's the firm became British agents for *Scrib-
ner's Magazine* and later the *Century Magazine* and also acted as
agents for many of Smith, Elder & Company's publications,
among which were the works of Thackeray, whose books,
although largely unread today, were very popular in Victorian
days. This period also saw the opening of a branch establish-
ment of the Company in New York, which naturally helped to
widen its business interests and secure American copyright as
necessary. A more detailed account of the New York office will
be found elsewhere in this book (p. 16).

For many years Warne's were also the English agents for
the *St Nicholas Magazine* for children, which was published
in America. It was here that appeared in serial form Frances
Hodgson Burnett's famous story *Little Lord Fauntleroy* which
became so highly successful when later published in book form.
Although the great days of this book have perhaps gone for
ever in this country, it may be of interest to know that quite a
remarkable sale for the story was achieved by a French publisher who issued an illustrated translation in Paris in recent
years.

From "Nonsense Omnibus" by Edward Lear

"LORD FAUNTLEROY, MY LORD"

Drawing by H. M. Brock

It was during this Victorian period of the firm's history that Frederick Warne published several notable works which helped to develop an important section of the catalogue still with us today. We refer particularly to those books dealing with natural history and nature subjects generally. Outstanding among the earlier titles published were the following:

> *Flowering Plants, Grasses, Sedges and Ferns of Great Britain,* in 4 volumes, by Anne Pratt, edited and revised by Edward Step, F.L.S.
> *Favourite Flowers of Garden and Greenhouse,* in 4 volumes, by Edward Step, F.L.S.
> *The Royal Natural History,* in 6 volumes, edited by Richard Lydekker, B.A., F.R.S., F.G.S. Illustrated with 72 colour plates and upwards of 1,600 wood engravings.
> *Wild Life of the World—A descriptive survey of Geographical Distribution of Animals,* by Richard Lydekker, B.A., F.R.S., F.G.S., with over 600 illustrations and 120 studies in colour.
> *Every Man his Own Horse Doctor; Every Man his Own Cattle Doctor; The Sheep Doctor,* all by George Armatage, M.R.C.V.S.

Many of these volumes were very handsome even by today's standards, with the colour plates and production generally of a high order for the times. We have been told that the Lydekker volumes are still consulted by readers and students in view of their range and scope, particularly on the illustration side.

Many semi-religious novels, so popular in Victorian days, were also added to the catalogue and met with large sales, while many novels and stories by Frances Hodgson Burnett and Silas Hocking were also published. The latter writer's novel *Her Benny* was an extremely popular title and sold in tens of thousands for many years.

Of the books for children, special mention may be made of such series as Warne's Large Picture Toy Books and Aunt Louisa's London Toy Books, which were famous in their day. The Company often used the name Aunt Louisa in a series title and it also served on occasions as a pseudonym for a Mrs Valentine, who was Frederick Warne's editress in the early days and in fact the only female member of his staff at that time. Louisa was Mrs Warne's name and was chosen for that reason.

We should like to end this review of Frederick Warne's Victorian publications with the following list, from an early catalogue, of Warne's Popular Tracts for Working and Cottage Homes. They sold in their tens of thousands at the time but would no doubt hardly commend themselves to the progressive minds of today:

FOR WORKING HOMES

1. *My Pence; or What ought I to Do?*
2. *My Words; or, What ought I to Say?*
3. *My Minutes; or, How shall I Spend Them?*
4. *My Neighbours; or, How shall I Treat Them?*
5. *My Faults; or, Why am I Blamed?*
6. *My Duties; or, Why was I Made?*
7. *My Lot; or, What have I Received?*
8. *My Vows; or, What have I Promised?*
9. *My Way; or, Where am I Going?*
10. *My Home; or, Where shall I live?*
11. *My Bible; or, How should I Read It?*
12. *My Closet; or, How should I Pray?*

FOR COTTAGE HOMES

1. *The Daughter; or, Household Work.*
2. *The Sister; or, Influence for Good.*
3. *The Friend; or, Life's Companions.*
4. *The Wife; or, Cottage Comforts.*
5. *The Mother; or, New Ties.*
6. *The Step-Mother; or, An Open Heart.*
7. *The Teacher; or, Early Lessons.*
8. *The Worshipper; or, Sabbath Duties.*
9. *The Nurse; or, Anxious Watchings.*
10. *The Mourner; or, Hours of Sorrow.*
11. *The Mother-in-Law, or, Household Peace.*
12. *The Grandmother; or, The Family Crown.*

We reserve the final word on books, however, to what one might call a misadventure. Idly glancing through a collection of Sherlock Holmes stories in the World's Classics series, we

suddenly caught sight of a familiar name in the Introduction—
Frederick Warne. It appeared that in 1886 the young Dr Conan
Doyle had hawked his first Sherlock Holmes story round the
London publishers, including Warne's, and had had the work
duly returned with regrets. Here indeed was a fish which
somebody left to drop back into the water. A pity, it seemed, that
the great detective and his friend Dr Watson would never
again call at 15 Bedford Street.

As the old century drew to its close, with the Company now
an established name among London's publishers and the
founder's sons settled in the family business, old Frederick
Warne himself must have been equally aware of the passing of
the years. He still went down to the office in Bedford Street
from Bedford Square twice a day in an old four-wheeled cab,
frequently calling out to the cabby—"No smoking on duty,
John". In 1894, however, he finally retired from active business
life and continued to live at 8 Bedford Square until his death on
7th November 1901. He was buried at Highgate Cemetery, in
north London.

"The Owl and the Pussycat"
by Edward Lear

CHAPTER 3

The New York Branch

In 1881, fifteen years after the founding of the parent house, Mr
P. C. Leadbeater accompanied Mr Frederick Warne to New
York with a view to establishing a branch of the firm in that
city.

Office and warehouse were first established in that year at
Lafayette Place with Mr Leadbeater in charge. Since the warehouse was on one of the upper floors shipments had to be hauled
up with block and tackle and taken in through the window.

With the growth of the city, business moved up-town and
the firm moving with the trend later occupied premises in turn
at Cooper Union, 103 Fifth Avenue, East 22nd Street, Madison
Avenue, and 210 Fifth Avenue.

The Company prospered and on 29th March 1920 the Com-
pany Charter was filed and the firm became Frederick Warne
& Co. *Ltd*. The directors of the Company the first year were
P. C. Leadbeater, Rupert S. Hughes and E. G. Dumahaut.

The title of the firm was changed again in 1930 when the
Ltd was changed to the American *Inc*.

Mr Leadbeater directed the New York house for forty years,
until his retirement in 1921 when he was succeeded by Mr E. G.
Dumahaut who had been associated with the business for many
years.

In 1921 Mr Treble, who had been with the English house
since 1906, was transferred to New York. He succeeded Mr
Dumahaut in 1930 and remained head of the firm until his
retirement in 1956.

There is considerable difference between the activities of the
two houses, for whereas the English house is perhaps better
known for its wide range of general publications the name of the
American firm will always be associated with fine children's
books. When the late Frederick Melcher decided to present a
medal to the illustrator of the best picture book of the year he
had no hesitation in calling it the Caldecott Medal.

The Kate Greenaway Picture Books have been the inspiration of many products such as dresses, china, buttons, etc., and of course "Peter Rabbit", which unfortunately was not copyrighted in the United States, sponsored innumerable items from Peter Rabbit Handkerchiefs to Peter Rabbit Stores.

Also the relation of the American house with public libraries and kindred institutions is much closer and much more important than in Britain. The long life of many Warne picture books is largely due to the continued and increasing use of them in public libraries and schools throughout the country.

Mr Treble was rather amused on one occasion when a Boston bookseller said to him, "You know, Warne's get more out of their plates than any other house I know". Since the Caldecott, Greenaway, Crane, Brooke and Lear Books, to mention only a few, were all more than fifty years old at that time, he had a point.

With the growing population and the increased emphasis on education the demand for good books is growing rapidly and the New York house looks forward with confidence to the time when it will celebrate its one hundredth anniversary.

With the extremely high rentals in mid-town New York, many publishing houses have returned to lower Fifth Avenue and it is interesting to note that in 1963 Frederick Warne & Co. Inc. moved to 101 Fifth Avenue next door to the premises they occupied in 1900. The New York house is now in the care of Mr Richard Billington, son of the late Managing Director of Frederick Warne & Co. Ltd, London. He took charge on the retirement of Mr. A. L. Treble who still retains his directorship and visits New York each month.

From "The Tale of Samuel Whiskers" by Beatrix Potter

CHAPTER 4

Kate Greenaway and Randolph Caldecott

The world over the name of Kate Greenaway holds the mystery and magic of a familiar fairy tale in many a household and in those libraries and schools and bookshops where her picture books have been cherished and freshly explored by one generation after another.

Once in a hundred years I like to think the golden key to the kingdom of childhood unlocks the door for a rare creative spirit, who, in pictures or words, records what is seen and felt with a truth and beauty that defy time and space.

It was a purely visionary world that William Blake recorded for the eighteenth century in his *Songs of Innocence*. It was a very human world in which real children dance and play and sing in sunlit streets and gardens or beside the sea that Kate Greenaway recorded for the nineteenth century in *Under the Window* and *Marigold Garden*.

Clear memory of the wonder of her own happy childhood in country and city was behind these essentially English scenes. It is said that "K.G.", as she was familiarly known in her own time, never forgot the colour or form of anything she had looked upon in childhood. She seems to have been born with the rare sense of colour and design which has distinguished her work as the pioneer among picture books of a new order.

Twenty years after the publication of *Under the Window*, hailed in France, Germany, Holland, Belgium and the United States, almost as soon as in England, for its originality and truth to child life, Kate Greenaway wrote in a letter to Ruskin with whom she had corresponded during all that time:

"There are not any very good children's books about just now that I have seen. The rage for copying mine seems over, so I suppose someone will soon step to the front with something new. Children often don't care a bit about the books people think they will and I think they often like grown-up

PLATE 3

From *The History of John Gilpin* by William
Cowper, illustrated by Randolph Caldecott

From "Under the Window" by Kate Greenaway

books—at any rate I did. From Kenny Meadows' pictures to Shakespeare I learnt all the plays when I was very young indeed. It is curious how much the pictures can tell you— like the plays without words. I suppose I asked a good deal about them and was told and read little bits. I never remember when I didn't know what each play was about."

"That letter removes Kate Greenaway from the school of the Precious and the Quaint," declared the friend with whom I had shared it. "I had never dreamed she cared so much for Shakespeare or that she ever visited a bookshop. How little we know about her as a person!"

Turning the pages of my well-worn copy of *Kate Greenaway*, by M. H. Spielmann and G. S. Layard (Adam and Charles Black, London 1905), I told of Kate Greenaway's visit to a bookshop at Hastings and how she stood by while a lady who had asked for Kate Greenaway's books was shown several. "Are those all by Kate Greenaway?" the lady asked. The bookseller assured her that they were. Kate Greenaway was near enough to see that not one of them was her work but apparently she did not disclose her identity.

And then I read another of the revealing letters she wrote from London to her friend at Brantwood in the English Lake Country.

"Do you like the sound of things in the street? They want

a

to get up a society to suppress the noises—they ask me to belong and seem to think it very funny when I said I liked them. I feel so cheerful when I hear an organ playing nice lively tunes. I love a band, I like seeing the Salvation Army marching along and singing. I like the sound of the Muffin' Bell, for I seem again a little girl coming home from school in the winter afternoon. . . . I like the flower-sellers and the fruit stores and the sound of church bells. I should not like silence always. It is often when I've had enough of silence I go into the cheerful streets and find it a rest.''

Unfortunately the beautiful work by Spielmann and Layard from which the letters are quoted has been out of print for many years.

As one who had the good fortune to receive it as a gift in the year it was published I have valued it not only as a mine of information concerning Kate Greenaway herself from earliest childhood but also for the light it sheds upon the adventurous publishing of the last quarter of the nineteenth century when English picture books were the most beautiful in the world.

It also records a spirited skit in the Kate Greenaway manner by Randolph Caldecott which tells more of the friendship and fine humorous understanding which existed between the two artists than pages of text could tell. The story goes that Caldecott who was a guest at the same country house where Kate Greenaway was staying came down one morning declaring he had lost all power of working in his own style and that everything came out Kate Greenaway's. Miss Greenaway was so delighted with the sketch that she kept it as long as she lived.

At the height of her own great popularity she wrote to Mr Frederick Locker: "I've been to call on the Caldecotts today with Mrs Evans. My brother showed me some of Mr Caldecott's new drawings yesterday at Racquet-Court. They are so uncommonly clever (Hey Diddle-Diddle), The Dish running away with the Spoon—You can't think how much he has made of it. I wish I had such a mind.''

Kate Greenaway was always learning and although she could not be diverted from her own "lay", as Stacy Marks characterized it, telling her to stick to it in the face of Ruskin's

"*The Three Jovial Huntsmen*"
by Randolph Caldecott

strong pleas for "more realism", she was constantly feeding her imagination with the work of artists she admired. She was rarely fortunate in the friendships which grew out of genuine appreciation of her work and of the strong but retiring personality behind it.

Many of her happiest hours were spent in the company of Frederick Locker, in his home at Rowfant in Sussex, at Cromer, by the sea, or in the picture galleries and out-of-the-way shops of London. Mr Locker was an ardent bibliophile and collector who was well known in the London of his day as a writer of verse and a man of discriminating taste. The affection Kate Greenaway came to feel for him and his family is expressed in many letters and drawings and in the dedication of *Little Ann*, her own selection from the poems of Ann and Jane Taylor.

Her individual portraits of the four Locker children look out from one of the most carefully designed and executed of her books. From the letters exchanged we learn that Kate Greenaway played hockey with the Locker children and fully entered into their high spirits whenever she visited them.

From "Kate Greenaway's Birthday Book"

PLATE 4

From *Mother Goose* by Kate Greenaway

It is probable that Kate Greenaway and Caldecott often met since both were contributors to *The Graphic*, to *Little Folks* and to Routledge's *Christmas Annual*. One of the many legends that gathered about Kate Greenaway (who was often believed to be a man) was that she was the wife of Randolph Caldecott.

That there was spiritual kinship between the two artists who were born in the same month of the same year—Kate Greenaway 17th March and Randolph Caldecott on 22nd March 1846—the record stands clear in picture books utterly different in conception and execution yet alike in the simple intention to give pure joy to children in the England both knew and loved so well.

Caldecott looked through the eyes of William Cowper when he drew his matchless pictures for *John Gilpin's Ride*, published in 1878, the first of his sixteen picture books.

Kate Greenaway looked with her own eyes at the children she had seen in garden, village or farm, in London streets or beside the sea, and wrote verses to accompany them without apparently realizing that she was making a notable picture book. She had been told by Mr William Marcus Ward for whose house she had designed Christmas cards and valentines that her verses were "rubbish and without any poetic feeling", but although she unhesitatingly accepted Mr Ward's expert opinion on her drawings and destroyed those he considered bad she reserved the right to set down her thoughts in her own way, and continued to do so until she had made a collection of fifty or more. These she took to Edmund Evans, the colour printer, who had published the toy books of Walter Crane and was beginning to publish those of Caldecott.

Mr Evans had known John Greenaway, the father of Kate, a well-known wood engraver and draughtsman of the time who had been assistant engraver to Ebenezer Landells, the originator of *Punch*, to whom Mr Evans was apprenticed as a boy.

"I was fascinated with the originals of the drawings and the ideas of the verses," he said, "so I at once purchased them and determined to reproduce them in a small volume. The title, *Under the Window*, was selected afterwards from one of the first lines. At the suggestion of George Routledge & Sons I took the drawings and verses to Frederick Locker, the author of *London*

Drawing by Randolph Caldecott

Lyrics. . . . Locker was very much taken with the drawings and verses and showed them to Mrs Locker with quite a gusto; he asked me many questions about her and was evidently interested in what I told him of her. I do not think he did anything to improve the verses nor did K.G. herself. . . .

"After I had engraved the blocks and colour blocks I printed the first edition of 20,000 volumes and was ridiculed by the publishers for risking such a large edition of a six-shilling book; but the edition sold before I could reprint another edition; in the meantime copies were sold at a premium. Reprinting kept on until 70,000 was reached." French and German editions brought the numbers up to 100,000 copies or more. *Under the Window* was published in 1878.

Everything about *Under the Window* was fresh and different from any picture book that had been seen before—the lovely cover design, the pictorial title-page, the unique table of contents, reproducing in miniature and in colour the figures from each complete drawing in the book.

No one who had known the book in childhood seems to have forgotten its form or any of its pictures. And what a variety of activities and sheer nonsense appear ranging from the Five Little Sisters standing in a row in their big hats with their muffs, the supercilious Prince Finikin sipping tea with his mamma in the garden of his castle, the children just let out of school, the Proud Girl that struts about to the sheer loveliness of the Maying Party with their baskets of wildflowers and flowering branches.

"Children like something that excites their imagination—a very real thing mixed up with a great unreality like Bluebeard", Kate Greenaway wrote in a letter regarding an exhibition of pictures for children that was to be held at the Fine Art Society in December 1899. She expresses doubt that children will appreciate the exhibition. "I often notice that they don't at all care for what grown-up people think they will", and recalls how thrilled she used to be by "Sister Ann, Sister Ann!" done in the agonized voice of Bluebeard's wife. "I could hardly breathe when the stains would not come off the key."

"Those wonderful little books they used to sell in coloured covers, a penny and a half-penny each. They were all deeply fascinating but I think I liked best *The Sleeping Beauty in the Wood, Cinderella* and *Beauty and the Beast.* It would be curious to do a book of them from one's remembrance of them in one's early thoughts. I know my Bluebeard people were not dressed as Turks then."

Such observations indicate how keenly aware Kate Greenaway was of the changing patterns in the field of art in the 1890's. And how firmly rooted in childhood as an unchanging element in human life was her way of seeing and recording what she felt when she looked.

"You can go into a beautiful new country if you stand under an apple tree and look up to the blue sky through the white flowers—to go to this scented land is an experience", she wrote

From "Marigold Garden" by Kate Greenaway

in 1896. "I suppose I went to it very young before I could really remember and that is why I have such a wild delight in cowslips and apple-blossom. They always give me the same strange feeling of trying to remember, as if I had known them in a former world.

"I always feel Wordsworth must have felt that a little too—when he wrote 'The Intimations of Immortality'—I mean the trying to remember. It's such a beautiful world, especially in the spring."

*   *   *

I visited the children's rooms of several branches of the New York Public Library, where I learned at first hand that in circulation for reading at home, as well as in the reading-rooms in the Library, Kate Greenaway holds a place of her own.

Of the many ABC books published in recent years *A-Apple Pie* is by far the most popular with the children of the libraries. *Kate Greenaway's Mother Goose* has not been superseded by any of the moderns in the eyes of those who are looking for a little one of perfect design.

Under the Window, *Marigold Garden* and *The Pied Piper* are still without rivals and are better known and loved today than they were twenty-five years ago.

The Book of Games circulates freely, and *The Queen of the Pirate Isle* still has an interest for children who are able to read Bret Harte's romantic story of California mining days. The Chinese boy, who is the real hero, and the miners dressed up as pirates presented a challenge to Kate Greenaway which she met on a more realistic plane than was usual with her. I recall an enthusiastic review of this book by Eric Kelly when it was reprinted in 1931. He had read it when a small boy living in Denver, Colorado, and had clearly remembered both story and pictures.

That boys, as well as girls, enjoy Kate Greenaway's pictures and frequently join the groups to which the verses are being read I was told at each of the children's rooms I visited. This did not surprise me for boys care quite as much about flowers and gardens and often bring a keener appreciation for the background of a picture than do girls.

From "The Language of Flowers"
by Kate Greenaway

At the exhibition of old valentines held every year in the Central Children's Room, New York, it is the boys who take the greater interest in the delicate workmanship and in the ideas presented in "The Language of Flowers" by which Kate Greenaway is always represented in this exhibition. The Almanacks also are studied with admiration and *The Birthday Book* is a never failing source of pleasure. One of the East Side libraries has among its treasures a copy of *The Birthday Book* in which children who came from Russia, Poland, Armenia, Italy, Germany and other foreign lands wrote their names during a celebration of Kate Greenaway's birthday.

Kate Greenaway seemed very much alive to these children with whom "The Big Blue Book" about her (Spielmann and Layard) had been shared. They liked to hear of the Punch and Judy and other shows she used to see with her sister in London streets, of the plays her father took her to see at the theatre; of the farm in the country where she rode to market in a green cart drawn by a brown pony and where she came to know so many of the flowers they could see in her books. They liked to know she went to the seaside and the fairy tales she liked best; they were often favourites of their own. They laughed at the nickname, "Knocker", her father gave her, and they were interested to know that he was an artist who sometimes had to work all night over a picture for *The Illustrated London News*. At such times little K.G. would go to bed with all her clothes on to be ready to get up and give him a cosy breakfast before anyone else in the house was stirring.

Children are quick to build up a personality out of a few bits of real information which fit in with their own experience.

In each one of the libraries I visited I was told of the perennial interest in dressing up and in copying the hats and bonnets and dresses of the grown-ups in the Greenaway books. Impersonating the characters was often noted. At a library in Greenwich Village, New York City, it was remembered that a resourceful child had cut the bottom from a paper bag, put a string through it and hung the bag from her neck, while she paraded up and down the sidewalk, hands thrust through the bag, in imitation of her favourite picture—"Girl with a Muff". At another time a Kate Greenaway tea-party was observed on the sidewalk. Two little girls were gravely seated at a packing case they had brought from the grocery shop on the corner, intent on carrying out the whole picture.

"It is to the picture books of Caldecott and Kate Greenaway we turn instinctively when asked for books to give children an idea of what England is really like", said more than one of the children's librarians who shared their experiences with me.

And then I knew I had come full circle back to my own first introduction of the two artists in the Children's Room of the Pratt Institute Free Library in Brooklyn, N.Y., fifty years ago. Picture books were few in number at that time. France and Germany were represented, American picture books had not been born, but it was there and then that I came to a realization of the importance of picture books in creating international relationships of an enduring kind.

From: *A Century of Kate Greenaway*
by ANNE CARROLL MOORE

CHAPTER 5

The Sons, 1895-1918

Following the retirement of Frederick Warne in 1895, the control of the business passed into the hands of his three sons, Harold, Fruing and Norman. Harold, the eldest of the three, was a strong character and a clever and able man who had a flair for what he called the middle class of children's books. As events turned out, many of these books, with the passing years, have been recognized as first class both in content and production. Almost at the outset of the period under review Leslie Brooke, for instance, who was just beginning his career as an illustrator, suggested to the Company the idea of an illustrated book of nursery rhymes, which finally appeared with his drawings in 1896, edited by Andrew Lang. From that time onwards Mr Brooke published his work regularly with Warne's and his illustrated books for children, particularly the Johnny Crow books for instance, became firm favourites both here and in America. A short review of his work generally is to be found in the present volume (p. 40).

The year 1902 saw the publication by Warne's of *The Tale of Peter Rabbit* and the commencement of Beatrix Potter's long association with the Company. The story of Miss Potter's many

From "The Tale of Pigling Bland" by Beatrix Potter

attempts to get the story accepted by various London publishers and its final publication by Warne's is now general knowledge and is dealt with in greater detail in the article on p. 47 of this volume. We can, however, recall an old member of the Company's warehouse staff, Mr "Buster" Brown, who always maintained he could remember seeing Miss Potter on her first visit to 15 Bedford Street, waiting nervously in the showroom for her interview with her prospective publishers. It struck him, so he told us, that she almost seemed on the point of walking out of the shop, so that he asked her if she was being attended to and she replied that she hoped so. Nothing loath, and wishing to be helpful, "Buster", a young man at the time, went and reminded the office staff of their visitor who was still waiting. He always hoped that he had added his small quota to the Beatrix Potter saga and that but for his timely remark she might have fled never to return.

Perhaps it may be fitting here to mention the youngest of the three brothers, Norman Dalziel Warne, who encouraged Beatrix Potter in her early published work, became in turn her friend and admirer and finally was engaged to marry her before his untimely death in 1905 from pernicious anaemia. Miss Potter was a frequent visitor to the Warne home at Bedford Square, where Norman lived with his parents and his sister Milly, and the two young women soon became friendly. In his spare time Norman built a doll's house for his brother's children, and Beatrix Potter depicted it in her *Tale of Two Bad Mice*. He was a keen cyclist and was fond of an early morning bathe in the Serpentine of London's Hyde Park, often taking with him his young nephew Fred (Frederick Warne Stephens of the present Company) who started work at 15 Bedford Street on 1st June 1903. Although Norman worked to a considerable extent on the book production side of the business, he also did some travelling on the Company's behalf and his early loss was deeply felt at the time.

The other son of the founder, William Fruing Warne, was mainly concerned with the sales side of the business, carrying on a daily correspondence with the firm's representatives when not travelling himself and continuing in this capacity in the business until his appointment as Managing Director of the

PLATE 5

From *The Three Bears* by L. Leslie Brooke

limited company in 1919. The older booksellers of Birmingham, Liverpool and Manchester, among others, will possibly still remember this genial man, who was both a good salesman and one of the best and most friendly of representatives. He used to work Leeds, Bradford and Halifax in a week and anyone following him had his work cut out to equal his timetable and his sales figures. He also visited Australia, New Zealand and India in the service of the Company.

Like his brother Harold, he was a devoted family man and charming to his friends and the staff at Bedford Street.

It was during the early years of the new century that another subsequently better-known author began to make his mark at Warne's in quite a different sphere from children's books. This was Edward Step, the naturalist, whose early titles in the Wayside and Woodland series set a new standard in practical handbooks on nature subjects intended for the general reader. The first one, *Wayside and Woodland Blossoms*, was followed by a number of others from the same author until the series became generally established in the catalogue as standard works of their kind. Later additions to the series such as *Moths of the British Isles* by Richard South and *Birds of the British Isles* by T. A. Coward have now become classics on their respective subjects, both for the authority of the texts and the wide range of illustrations given.

A few words may be of interest here regarding Edward Step, F.L.S., who was Warne's reader and editor for many years. A keen botanist and entomologist, he was a hard and diligent worker whose accuracy was rarely in question. He first joined the Linnean Society in 1896, became President of the South London Entomological Society and of the British Naturalists' Association and was a member of the Lambeth Field Club, where he was a popular and admired leader of natural history rambles. Many of his books were illustrated largely from his own photographs and with drawings by his eldest daughter Mabel. Of his own ambition in life he wrote (and we quote his own words): "From his youth onward, he tried to extend the knowledge of biological facts by translating the researches of the specialist into the vulgar idiom." He died in 1931, three days before his seventy-sixth birthday.

Returning to our story of the house of Warne, it thus appeared that within the first few years of the new partnership the broad outlines of the firm's publishing policy set a pattern which was to serve it well for many years ahead. The effects are still with us today, if one considers that the books of Leslie Brooke and Beatrix Potter are still loved and read and are at the same time typical of the kind of children's books Warne's strive to produce, while the Wayside and Woodland series, considerably augmented and revised as they are from earlier days, have in their turn formed the original germ of the Observer's Books, the first of whose titles were based on earlier Wayside volumes.

From "The Tale of Pigling Bland" by Beatrix Potter

Coincidentally with this publishing trend, several of the staff who had joined Warne's either just before or soon after the year 1900 remained to leave their mark on the affairs of the Company for many years afterwards. For the sake of the record we mention them here:

Mr Frederick Warne Stephens, a grandson of the founder, started with the Company in 1903 as previously mentioned, and became eventually its overseas representative, visiting Australia, New Zealand and South Africa annually, with an occasional trip to India and the Far East. Mr Stephens later became a Director and finally Chairman of the Company until the end of 1964.

Mr W. Herring joined the Company in 1894 from Dalziel's, and was for many years Production Manager. He saw Beatrix

Potter's and Leslie Brooke's publications through the press as well as being actively concerned in the production of the Wayside and Woodland volumes. Mr Herring later became a Director of the Company.

Mr Arthur Emery began work with the firm in 1899 after two years in Malaya, and became cashier in 1907, continuing in this responsible post until his retirement in 1945.

Finally we mention Mr T. C. Opher and Mr Arthur Treble who commenced with Warne's in 1898 and 1906 respectively. Mr Opher later became the Suburban traveller (following on Mr A. G. Dryden) until his retirement in 1944, while Mr Treble was transferred to the New York office in 1921 and tells his own story on p. 16 in this book.

It must not of course be forgotten that while these men were coming to the fore, there were already several older-serving members who had started in the 1880's and possibly earlier who were also to be active in the Company's affairs until at least up to the mid-1930's—men such as Mr Harry Messenger of the Binding Department, Mr "Tommy" Webb of the Country Department, and Mr "Teddy" Barnard, the Town traveller, as well as a number of loyal warehousemen and packers who had served the firm faithfully as far as their abilities allowed.

Regarding "Teddy" Barnard—whose adventure with the top-hats we have previously referred to—he was quite a definite character who worked continuously from the mid-1880's until 1944, when he retired. As the Company's Town traveller, his hearty and distinctive laugh and shining bald head, to say nothing of the occasional pinch of snuff, must have been known and recognized over the length and breadth of the City book trade. As time went by, it appeared as if he had not only known most of his customers from boyhood, but had also called on their fathers before them, so long was he in the trade. His cheery "Hallo, old darlin'!" to all and sundry, especially on the telephone, must have been long remembered. He commuted daily from Worcester Park, Surrey, first going there in the pre-1914 era when residents were comparatively rare. It was rumoured that in those far-off days of steam, the engine-driver would not only give him a friendly "toot" across the fields, but would wait for him at the station if he were late. Any traveller on that busy crowd-thronged line today could no doubt tell a different story.

Concerning staff conditions generally in Edwardian times, it must be borne in mind that the Company was a small private family partnership with a total staff of some forty-five to fifty persons, of whom not more than the odd one or two were women. In these circumstances, although working hours were longer than today's, and Saturday work until perhaps the early afternoon was the normal thing (and the men's weekly pay was not ready until then) the atmosphere was a friendly and personal one between partners and staff. This no doubt explains the continuity of service and the staff loyalty over the years.

Of the books published by the partners, those of Beatrix Potter and Leslie Brooke were the most important titles for children. Although the last Beatrix Potter book was not to appear until 1930, the majority were already published by 1914 and her name was well-established, even if her fame since then has tended to underline and enhance that early popularity. Of her original illustrations, it may interest the reader to know that the Company hold those of *Peter Rabbit*, that the drawings for *The Tailor of Gloucester* are in the London Tate Gallery where they are normally on view, while the "Flopsy Bunnies" illustrations are in the Prints and Drawings Department of the British Museum. Others are held by the National Trust at the artist's former home of Hill Top, Sawrey, near Ambleside. Miss Potter's original art work has a delicate charm very difficult to capture in reproduction and her admirers are advised to avail themselves of any opportunity to see her actual drawings when exhibited.

On a lower plane, there was any amount of juvenile fiction published by Warne's over this period of the partnership, and known in the trade as Reward Books. These were largely adventure and school stories, illustrated in the manner of the times, with plenty of gilt lettering and vignetted blocking to the binding cases to attract the younger reading public—the modern colourful book jacket or laminated cover was as yet unknown.

PLATE 6

'*And the Lion had a green and yellow Tie on*'

From *Johnny Crow's Garden* by
L. Leslie Brooke

"Come Lassies and Lads", drawing by Randolph Caldecott

For adult readers the Company published *Our Home Railways* by W. J. Gordon in 1910, a two-volume, lavishly illustrated review of the subject at a time when the railways were the only form of fast transport and Britain was served by a host of independent railway companies instead of the all-embracing British Railways of today. These volumes have in recent times been re-issued by Messrs Ian Allan Ltd as among the "classics" of railway literature.

In pre-1914 days there were also an extraordinary number of standard literary anthologies and works, published by the Company over a period of years, and for which there was presumably a market. There was a twelve-volume set of *Cameos of Literature from Standard Authors*, there were *Half Hours of English History* in four volumes, *Half Hours with the Best Authors* in four volumes, *Half Hours with the Best American Authors* in four volumes, and so on, while such classics as *Mrs Hemans' Poetical Works*, *Lowell's Poetical Works*, *Gems of National Poetry* and Motley's *Rise of the Dutch Republic* found their place in the catalogue alongside Byron, Milton and Shakespeare.

A feature of these publications was the remarkable and varied styles of binding available apparently from stock. We single out as an example the Lansdowne Pocket Edition of *Shakespeare* in six volumes. In language reminiscent of the prose

D

of Oscar Wilde's *Dorian Gray*, the bindings of this title were catalogued in 1913 as available in the following styles:

(1) Half-white cloth, with watered silk sides, richly gilt, in elegant folding watered silk box case.

(2) Venetian morocco, round corners, red under gold edges, gilt roll, in Venetian morocco folding case.

(3) Finest Turkey morocco, limp, red under gold edges, round corners, tooled borders, in best Turkey morocco-lined case, patent folding form.

(4) Full calf, red under gold edges, round corners, tooled borders, in full calf-lined case, patent folding form.

As far as we are aware, no publisher today—or binder either—could possibly manage this type of thing as a matter of general routine, and after all this refinement the most common binding for this title of "cloth gilt, in cloth case" rather lets one down with a bump. No doubt the war of 1914 and its aftermath put an end to all this elaboration, which was not necessarily confined to Warne's at the time.

During the First World War of 1914–18, the Company continued its normal business activity as far as war-time conditions permitted. There were naturally shortages on occasions and stock was not always available to fulfil all orders received, in which case a percentage was all that the bookseller could expect. Production standards too must have lowered gradually, as paper, print and binding failed to keep to their former pre-war quality.

Of the members of the staff serving overseas, mention must be made of Mr W. H. ("Billy") Greenwood, who had first come to the firm via Philip, Son & Nephew and his own business in Liverpool. As a Naval Volunteer, he elected to go overboard to relieve an overloaded boat after his ship had been torpedoed in the Mediterranean. Fortunately he was picked up later and in due course returned to his old place as the Trade Counter Manager, where he was a conscientious worker and kindness itself. It was typical of Billy that when his fellow-colleagues presented him with a set of gardening tools on his retirement in the 1930's, he jokingly remarked that he would rather they had subscribed to such a gift than have to send the hat round for a wreath for him. As a supplement at the end of this chapter we append a composition of Mr Greenwood, where, with great verve, he has crammed into a short address more titles from the Company's publications than we care to count. Written in 1910 we print it as a souvenir of a vanished era.

A number of the staff re-joined the Company at the end of the war in 1918, and together with those newcomers who had entered the business during this period, looked forward no doubt to a continuation of the life which the previous four years had interrupted. With the rising of prices and the uncertain conditions of the time, however, a return to the old order of the pre-1914 era was impossible. At Warne's the partners found themselves in deeper waters financially than a small private business was capable of steering through with success, and after a period of some difficulty a limited company was formed in 1919, with Mr Harry Wingfield as Chairman and financial adviser and Mr Fruing Warne as the first Managing Director. Mr Harold Warne, having now left the Company, in due course set up his own business in the stationery trade.

SUPPLEMENT TO THIS CHAPTER

The following ingenious oration was the work of Mr W. H. Greenwood of the Trade Counter. All the words or phrases in italics are book titles from Warne's catalogue of the period:

A few thoughts suggested by the departure of Mr Horace Woollett to Australia, spoken as a "send-off" at the Criterion Rooms, London, 4th November 1910.

"This morning, whilst sitting in *Johnny Crow's Garden,* just *Under the Window*—watching *Little Ann,* in her *Marigold Garden,* playing with *Tom Kitten,* a few thoughts came to my mind regarding Horace, who is being *Decoyed Across the Sea,* and will soon be leaving *The Abbeys, Castles and Ancient Halls of England and Wales.*

A desire has *Gripped His Great Self* to go *In Quest of Sheba's Treasure,* and, quite incidentally, of course, in search of more *Work and Wages*—so, like *The Heroes of the United Service,* he goes, as he thinks, *Where Duty Lies,* in the faith that he may earn *Ten Thousand a Year* by sending home frequent orders amounting to *Forty Thousand Pounds*, and, possibly, as *A Desperate Hope, The Hepsworth Millions*.

We are told that *The Pied Piper of Hamelin* so skilfully played upon his pipe, that he lured all who heard him to follow whithersoever he led—and in like manner (*A Sad Strange Comedy*) that *When Life is Young*, the desire for *The Power of Gold* should be far more fascinating than the *Quiet Stories* from an *Old Woman's Garden*, and certainly *Passing the Love of Women*.

However, the Horace of *British (Commercial) History of the Victorian Era* having been brought up in *The True Christian Religion*—not *Under the Red Rag of Ritual*—putting his trust in a not *Unknown God*, sets out with *The Wizard's Light* to meet *His Sombre Rivals* in business, equipped with a full range of samples, an all *Conquering Will* and his little *Torn Bible Near to Nature's Heart*.

No doubt, for a time, after arriving amongst the *Fragrant Flowers and Leaves* of that far-off land, he will be *Without a Home*, but in his journeys will find *The House in the Wood In the Shadow of the Hills*, a pleasant abiding place, where he and his *Dolly* can, *With Loving Hands*, arrange their *Chips* of furniture, place the *Cameos of Literature On the Shelf* and hang their gems from *The National Gallery* alongside *Paul Heriot's Pictures*—and in a very short time, instead of a *Racketty-Packetty House*, there will be one fit for a *Prince of the House of David*.

In following *Fortune's Tangled Skein*, he may feel that he for ever leaves *Picturesque England—Nobody Knows!* but I think in *The Ebb Tide* of life *Moods* will come, which will cause him to again turn *Westward Ho!* and we shall learn from *The Yellow Journalist* of the *Kings of the Sea* landing him safely in some *Englishman's Haven*, there to find himself, probably *Twenty Years After*, in the land of *His Father*, and of *Yours and Mine*,—and then, by the help of *Our Home Railways*, rushed back to this great city which clusters round *Old St Paul's*, here to endure such *Food and Feeding* on *Lamb's Tales* and *Roly-Poly Pudding*, washed down with dry-*Ginger and Pickles*, and later, at *Johnny Crow's Party* with the *Goblin*

Gobblers we have heard about, once more rapturously listening to the *Old Old Fairy Tales* and the strains of *The Pelican Chorus*.

But to come from *Jest to Earnest*, I think I shall be but uttering that which is in *Other Men's Minds* when I say our *Last Sentence* shall be to wish Mr Woollett and *His Duchess Lass* every success in their *Chase Round the World*, and that the *Net Profit Tables* will tell of business *Barriers Burned Away*, and that the house we have the pleasure of working in, and for— in short *The House we Live in*, will see such a *Dawn of a To-Morrow*, as will surprise, not only the *Captain General*, but *The Great Panjandrum Himself*.

From "*Nonsense Omnibus*"
by *Edward Lear*

CHAPTER 6

L. Leslie Brooke

The name of Leslie Brooke has been so much associated with the Warne imprint over the years—*Johnny Crow*, *The Golden Goose Book*, *Nonsense Songs* all being well-established favourites for several generations of children on both sides of the Atlantic —that it comes with an element of surprise to realize that he had already attained the modest age of two and was as a very small boy already fast approaching his third birthday, before the foundation of the house of Warne in mid-1865. Leonard Leslie Brooke, of Irish ancestry, was born at Birkenhead on 24th September 1862. This bare statement of fact may perhaps clear up a small doubt in some minds, as it once did in the present writer's, as to what the initial "L", which always preceded the "Leslie Brooke" on a title page, could possibly be an abbreviation for. We have no knowledge of at what stage in his career the Leonard was quietly dropped in favour of the Leslie Brooke we all know and appreciate, but he certainly grew up to manhood in the hey-day of Victorian England and his life spanned a period long enough to see his last book, *Johnny Crow's New Garden*, published in 1935 and the early days of the Second World War. He died at Hampstead, London, on May Day, 1940.

Leslie Brooke had trained in his younger days at the schools of the Royal Academy in London and became in time a portrait painter of some distinction before he established his now better-known career as an illustrator. He had done a certain amount of early work for publishers such as Blackie and Cassell's and had succeeded Walter Crane as illustrator of Mrs Molesworth's annual story for Macmillan's, but his first connection with Warne's began in the winter of 1895–6, when he suggested to them the idea of a new volume of nursery rhymes. As a result came the publication in 1897, of *The Nursery Rhyme Book* edited by Andrew Lang, with illustrations in black and white by Leslie Brooke. This book established both the artist's distinctive style and his continuous association with Frederick Warne as his publishers until the final Johnny Crow book in 1935.

From *"The Nursery Rhyme Book"*,
drawing by L. Leslie Brooke

Leslie Brooke had married his distant cousin Sybil, a daughter of the Reverend Stopford Brooke, in 1894, and for a number of years they lived at Harwell, then a quiet village near the Berkshire Downs. Here their two boys must have been among the very first fascinated explorers of the inimitable world of Johnny Crow, whose garden was visited by that motley and eccentric collection of animals which Leslie Brooke depicts with so much precision and humour. The book *Johnny Crow's Garden,* a picture book with a phrase or two of verse beneath each illustration, was dedicated to his two boys Leonard and Henry and was published by Warne's in 1903. It appears that the artist first heard of Johnny Crow from his own father and was encouraged to make a book of the bird's adventures at his wife's suggestion. We are happy to say that it has been in print ever since.

Although taking the title role, so to speak, and appearing in the solo part on the opening page of the book, Johnny Crow's presence thereafter is that of the tactful host, helping out as occasion demands, with the Crane's umbrella and the Beaver's indisposition—where he is to be found carrying a dish of light diet for the unhappy patient—and keeping an ever-watchful eye on the mouse whenever the cat is about, and so on to the final releasing of his animal guests from the clutches of the Fox, who had put them "in the stocks".

The book shows Leslie Brooke's style at its best: a quiet humour running through it all, a love of detail and a decided flair for animal drawing and expression, coupled with a draughtsmanship perhaps a little dated by today's standards, but nevertheless emphasizing the artist's care for his work and his personal integrity. No pen-and-ink line in a Leslie Brooke drawing is ever haphazard; it is always in its inevitable and correct place as the artist had seen it. His colour work too is based on what is fundamentally a pen-and-ink outline drawing, with the colours added as modelling or background wash to complete the picture. The effect is generally of a fresh watercolour style, the colour often applied very delicately.

Johnny Crow's Party, published in 1907, continued the story of that hero and his friends, with the garden again forming the main background to the party, marred for a time by the departure of the Cock and Hen (with family) who vowed they would "never come again", but recovering sufficiently by the time the chimpanzee "put the kettle on for tea", so that all ended happily. This book also became a great favourite with children.

Mention should be made here of another early Leslie Brooke classic—his illustrated edition of Edward Lear's *Nonsense Songs*—published in 1900 in two parts as *The Pelican Chorus* and *The Jumblies*. Edward Lear's own sketchy characteristic art work is so opposed to Leslie Brooke's painstaking draughtsmanship, that one wonders if the latter almost accepted Lear's nonsensical text as a challenge to be taken seriously—and illustrated seriously come what may. If so, Leslie Brooke succeeded admirably, investing such characters as "The Dong with the Luminous Nose" and "The Table and the Chair" with an actuality that can almost be believed in, while his illustrations for such old-tried favourites as "The Owl and the Pussy Cat", "The Jumblies" and the "Duck and the Kangaroo" are all of a high order. A new edition of *Nonsense Songs* was issued in one volume as recently as 1954, with new printing plates for the colour work, thus giving to the inspired nonsense of Lear and the drawings of Leslie Brooke a continued existence together into our own day.

One of Leslie Brooke's handsomest volumes, published in 1905 and still in print, is his *Golden Goose Book,* produced while the family were still living at Harwell and containing four well-known children's stories, illustrated in line and colour in the artist's finest style. Of all his work perhaps his interpretation of both "The Three Bears" and "The Three Little Pigs" is among the happiest. The whole series of drawings for both stories is full of deft touches of subtle humour, with the expressions of bears and pigs in each case being caught to the life, to say nothing of the masterly way in which the crafty wolf is depicted in the latter tale, foiled at every turn and realizing it, to the

"The Story of the Three Little Pigs"

intense satisfaction of the pig who had built his house of brick. The artist's final sketch of this particular porker, sitting beside his own fireside and smoking a pipe, is the very essence of

"The Story of the Three Little Pigs"

smugness and repletion combined, with the wolf's skin as a hearth-rug beneath his feet.

In 1910 the Brookes moved to London and this was to be the artist's home until 1922, in a charming house with a studio in St John's Wood. During the pre-1914 era he produced further work for publication—illustrations for a collection of old fairy stories under the title of *The House in the Wood* in 1909, then *The Truth about Old King Cole* in 1910 and *The Tailor and the Crow* in 1911, all the drawings enhancing the artist's growing reputation in both England and America. With the 1914–18 war came the loss of his elder son Leonard.

In 1922, four years after the end of war, he saw the publication in one large volume, as a companion to *The Golden Goose Book*, of a collection of favourite nursery rhymes under the general title of *Ring o' Roses*. The book was composed of four

separate groups of rhymes and pictures which had been published during previous years and were now brought together
between the same covers. Little Bo-Peep, Simple Simon,
Humpty Dumpty and the Pig that went to Market and many
other well-known characters were depicted in Leslie Brooke's
own inimitable manner. Many of the colour plates were particularly attractive in both design and delicacy of colouring.

A Roundabout Turn by Robert H. Charles, a tale in verse which
had originally appeared in *Punch*, of a toad wishing to see the
world, was issued with drawings by Leslie Brooke in 1930 and
is perhaps interesting as being one of the few instances where
any of his work referred to an actual place. The Albury Heath
of the story is near Guildford in Surrey. As a general rule he
relied on his own imagination for background scenery, differ-
ing in that respect from his famous contemporary Beatrix
Potter, whose work is inseparable from her own home and its
surroundings.

Leslie Brooke left London in 1922 to live in a house he built
in Cumnor, near Oxford. He had always been a keen walker
and no doubt on many a country ramble had studied farm
animals with pencil and sketch pad at the ready, making
copious notes and drawings to be stored and memorized for
future use. He finally returned to London in 1934 to be near his
son Henry, who was living with his family at Hampstead, a
pleasant North London suburb which had in earlier days included Romney, Constable, Keats and Kate Greenaway among
its more distinguished residents. Of its many quiet Georgian
streets, the delightful Church Row is one of the most noted, and
in a house near here Leslie Brooke came to live.

Before leaving Cumnor he had completed the drawings for
his last book *Johnny Crow's New Garden*, which was published in
1935 and dedicated to his grandson Peter. When one considers
that his final Johnny Crow book was illustrated a full thirty
years after the first, their unity of atmosphere and draughtsmanship is quite remarkable. As in the two previous books,
misfortune comes to threaten the proceedings and on this
occasion it is the Weasels—"who caught the measles"—which
nearly upsets everything. Fortunately both Dr Goat and
Johnny himself are in attendance as usual and the colour

drawing of the two unfortunate sufferers tucked up in bed under the eye of both these stalwarts is one of the most delightful in the book and shows that Leslie Brooke even at the age of seventy had by no means lost his touch.

This book came as a fitting climax to the artist's distinguished career as an illustrator of children's books, with the traditional material of rhyme and story as the main foundation for his work. He will be especially remembered for his insight into animal character and delineation, together with a keen sense of humour and conscientious care for good drawing. All these qualities, combined with his obvious appreciation of the child's mind, have enabled his books to hold their place up to our own day and perhaps for time to come. His conscientiousness extended to seeing all his work through the press down to the last final detail and many letters to and from his publishers testify to his concern to see his work reproduced as faithfully as the printing methods of the time would allow. He was of that great tradition of artist-illustrators, both men and women, whose work over the past century has survived to the present day and Warne's are proud to have been associated with him in their mutual concern for producing good children's books.

"Johnny Crow"

CHAPTER 7

Beatrix Potter, 1866-1943

Beatrix Potter was born on 28th July 1866, and lived at No. 2 Bolton Gardens, London. Her parents were both well-to-do, having inherited their money from the Lancashire textile industry. Her grandfather, Edmund Potter, who married Jessy Crompton, was head of one of the largest calico printing works in Europe, and lived at Camfield Place, Hertfordshire, a stately country house with 300 acres of land. Beatrix Potter often stayed there and was devoted to her grandmother.

Her father, Rupert Potter, lived in retirement. He was a member of a number of London's most fashionable clubs and mixed in high society, knowing many distinguished people, amongst whom were John Bright the statesman, and Sir John Millais the painter. Rupert Potter was also friendly with Mr Gaskell, a Unitarian minister and husband of the well-known novelist.

Beatrix Potter's earliest childhood memories were associated with Camfield Place. She remembered as a child, lying in a crib in the nursery bedroom: "I used to be awakened at four in the morning by the song of the birds in the elm. I can feel the diamond pattern of that yellow crib against my cheek, as I lay with my head where my heels should be, staring backwards over my eyebrows at the plaster heads on the chimney-piece and a large water-colour alpine scene which I regarded with respectful awe."

Although the Potter family lived at No. 2 Bolton Gardens, London, a considerable part of each year was spent away from home. Because of her father's health, the Easter holidays were spent in Devonshire, Dorset or Cornwall. Many of the backgrounds depicted in her *Little Pig Robinson* were inspired by memories of these early holidays at such places as Ilfracombe, Falmouth, Weymouth and Sidmouth.

The summer months were spent in Scotland, where year-by-year, from the age of five until she was sixteen, her father rented

Dalguise House, a fishing seat on the river Tay. John Bright the statesman would often stay at Dalguise House; Sir John Millais the painter and Mr Gaskell were frequent visitors.

When Beatrix Potter was six, her brother Bertram was born. As he grew older, both children would spend many happy hours together during the school holidays, studying nature and looking after their innumerable pets—mice, birds, frogs, lizards, rabbits . . . and even snakes.

Beatrix Potter was a keen, alert and unusually observant child. Although she never went to school, she was fortunate in having a charming and sympathetic governess in the person of Miss Hammond. Miss Hammond loved the child, and realizing her exceptional gift for drawing and painting, and her inborn appreciation of nature and art, encouraged and helped her in every way.

When Beatrix Potter reached the age of sixteen, Miss Hammond told her parents that she had taught her all she could, and that she now felt the time had come for her to leave. After Miss Hammond left, Beatrix Potter had a visiting governess for French, and another one, Miss Annie Carter, for German. She was a little troubled as to whether the continuation of her studies would interfere with her opportunities for drawing and painting. "I can't settle to anything but my painting . . . I cannot rest, I must draw."

Beatrix Potter became extremely fond of Miss Carter, who taught her for just over two years, after which she married and became Mrs Moore. From now onwards, apart from French, Beatrix Potter continued her studies alone.

When in London, Beatrix Potter made a point of visiting all the important Exhibitions at the Royal Academy and other art galleries. She studied the pictures critically, and later reviewed those which appealed to her most.

When about fourteen years of age, Beatrix Potter invented a code-alphabet, which for the next fifteen years she used for the purpose of keeping a private Journal. From her early years she had wanted to be a writer, and towards the end of her life when mentioning this code-writing in a letter to her cousin Caroline Clark, she wrote: "When I was young I already had the itch to write, without having any material to write about." Thus,

From "The Tale of Ginger and Pickles"
by Beatrix Potter

in a quiet and unobtrusive manner she developed her powers of writing.

Beatrix Potter wrote with craftsmanship, and it is clear that here was a writer in the making. In this Journal there are first-hand accounts of the people she met, the current affairs of the day, and of her many and varied interests. There are gaps in the sequence of events, but there are also long periods of day-to-day entries.

From time to time Beatrix Potter had sold an occasional drawing, but it was not until 1890 that any of her work was actually published. An idea to sell a set of designs to the trade, arose from the success of some Christmas cards "Which were put under the plates at breakfast and proved a five-minute wonder. I referred to them the other day and found my uncle had forgotten their existence, but he stated with laughable inconsistency that any publisher would snap at them." So in May of that year, Beatrix Potter prepared a set of six designs and offered them to Marcus Ward for the sum of £6. Marcus Ward was chosen first, because she had toned the colours from one of their Almanacs. To her dismay, they came back by return of post.

The next publisher on her list was the German firm of Hildescheimer & Faulkner, who immediately recognized their merit and sent her a cheque for £6. This event caused great excitement. In due course the designs were issued, both as

Christmas and as New Year cards, each card bearing the initials H.B.P. (Helen Beatrix Potter).

For some years now, Beatrix Potter had been in the habit of sending picture-letters and story-letters to children she knew, and in particular, to the children of her last governess Mrs Moore. The original story of Peter Rabbit was sent to Noel Moore in a letter from "Eastwood", Dunkeld, in September 1893, and at the suggestion of Canon Rawnsley, a founder-member of the National Trust whom the Potters had met in the Lake District, Beatrix Potter borrowed this story-letter and made a little book out of it. This manuscript, each page illustrated by an accompanying line-drawing, was submitted to a number of publishers, including the firm of Frederick Warne, but alas it was not accepted. In the meantime, however, she had added a coloured frontispiece, and in December 1901 had had 250 copies of the book privately printed by a London printer of the name of Strangeways (followed in February 1902 by a second printing of 200 copies).

It so happened that although Frederick Warne had declined her first offer, they had written her a most courteous letter in reply, and she therefore decided to give them a copy of her privately printed edition, half hoping that they might re-consider her first offer. Frederick Warne did re-consider this project, and wrote again, this time offering to produce an edition of 5000 copies if she would provide *coloured* illustrations, adding with extreme caution, "Of course we cannot tell whether the work is likely to run to a second edition or not."*

Thus began a long and intimate association with the firm of Frederick Warne, resulting in one of the most remarkable series of children's books ever to be produced; books small enough to be easily handled by a child, and of a clarity of text and illustration which not only delighted children, but which appealed equally to grown-ups. There was a coloured picture on the one side, and just the right amount of written text on the other, each word being carefully chosen to convey the right meaning.

It was to Mrs Moore's children that the next two books were

* Due to rather heavy initial expenses it was finally decided to print a first edition of 6000 copies.

Plate 7

'*He suggested that they should fill the pocket-handkerchief with onions*'

From *The Tale of Benjamin Bunny*
by Beatrix Potter

Eastwood Dunkeld
Sep 4ᵗ 93

My dear Noel,
I don't know what to
write to you, so I shall tell you a story
about four little rabbits
whose names were—

Flopsy, Mopsy Cottontail

and Peter

They lived with their mother in a
sand bank under the root of a
big fir tree.

*The first page of Beatrix Potter's
letter to Noel Moore*

E

Title page illustration from
"The Tale of Peter Rabbit"

Title page illustration from
"The Tale of Jemima Puddle-Duck"

dedicated. *The Tailor of Gloucester* to Freda (also privately printed by Strangeways—500 copies, December 1902), and *The Tale of Squirrel Nutkin* to Norah.

Year-by-year further titles were added to the series, and by 1913 there were no less than nineteen. In 1914, *The Tale of Kitty-in-Boots*, which had already been set-up in type, was abandoned, no doubt due to the commencement of Word War I. Only one of the original water-colours was ever finished.

During the war and up to 1930, four more titles were added to the series, including the two rhyme books, *Appley Dapply's* and *Cecily Parsley's Nursery Rhymes*, which really belonged to the period 1902–05. During that period, Beatrix Potter became engaged to Norman Warne, and they worked together on the planning of *Appley Dapply*; to be in a large format with the pictures on one side and the rhymes on the other, within patterned borders. It was a great grief to Beatrix Potter when quite suddenly Norman Warne died. She put the rhyme book on one side and did not work on it again until 1917, when it was produced on a much smaller scale.

The late Mr W. A. Herring, of Warne's staff, who had supervised the printing of all Beatrix Potter's books, could remember her well; how she would drive up to Bedford Court in her carriage, and how they would discuss the various problems which arose. He told of the care with which she corrected her proofs, and how she spared herself nothing in the preparation of the very finest drawings, and if any of these did not satisfy her, they were entirely re-drawn. Sometimes she would use a difficult word, and her publishers would question its suitability, "Little Benjamin conversed in whispers". "Too hard" they said, but Beatrix Potter wrote in reply, " '*conversed*', children like a fine word occasionally". This particular sentence, however, was re-written, but when it came to "soporific" in *The Tale of the Flopsy Bunnies*, in spite of what her publishers said, Beatrix Potter was adamant and nothing would persuade her to give it up.

During the summer months of 1896, Mr Potter rented "Lakefield" (now 'Ees Wyke), a large country house in the village of Near Sawrey, in Lakeland, with spacious grounds overlooking Lake Esthwaite Water situated just behind Hill Top Farm. It was probably during this holiday that Beatrix Potter first became intimately acquainted with Hill Top.

In 1905 she bought Hill Top Farm with the intention of putting in someone to run it and of staying there frequently herself. Beatrix Potter built an extension to the farm-house, reserving the main part for her own use. Before long, however, she decided to make it her home, and it was here in the little village of Near Sawrey that some of her best books were written. The quaint old farm-house was depicted in *The Roly-Poly Pudding*, the lovely garden with its colourful flowers in *The Tale of Tom Kitten*, and the farmyard in *The Tale of Jemima Puddle-Duck*. The Village Store in Sawrey became the setting for *Ginger and Pickles*, while some of the cottages and gardens in the

Title page illustration from
"The Tale of Mr Jeremy Fisher"

Title page illustration from
"The Tale of Two Bad Mice"

village were used as backgrounds for *The Pie and the Patty-Pan*. *The Tale of Mr Tod* and *The Tale of Pigling Bland* have their setting in the countryside around Sawrey, while *The Tale of Johnny Town Mouse* is mainly associated with Hawkshead.

In October 1913, Beatrix Potter married William Heelis, a solicitor from Hawkshead, who on many occasions had acted as her agent when buying property in the Lake District. After their marriage they made their home at Castle Cottage, a converted farmhouse close to Hill Top. At the bottom of the garden, looking across the field where Ribby carried the butter and milk from the farm, Beatrix Potter could still see Hill Top Farm.

We now lose sight of Beatrix Potter the writer, and in her place have Mrs Heelis the farmer, and a very successful one at that. All through the war years life was hard, and there was much work to be done on the farm. In a letter to Milly Warne she wrote, "I seldom sit down except to meals, the farm has done well with good crops in spite of the very wet season, but labour is a great anxiety."

As the years passed by, and as opportunity arose, Beatrix Potter bought land with a view to the preservation of the Lake District for the nation: she even sent some of her drawings to America to be sold for this purpose. Eventually she bequeathed to the National Trust about half the village of Near Sawrey, as well as other properties including a large part of Troutbeck Park Farm, one of the most famous sheep farms in the Lake District.

Although Beatrix Potter's new home was at Castle Cottage, Mrs Storey, who lives at Hill Top, and remembers her well, tells how she loved her old home best, and how during the last few years of her life she would often come round to Hill Top, arranging and sorting her papers and other treasured possessions. Said Mrs Storey, "She liked to come and go unnoticed, and to be left quite alone with her memories of the past; and I would never come into that part of the house when Mrs Heelis was there, although on cold, dark, winter afternoons, I often wished I could bring in cups of hot tea or cocoa to warm her."

Beatrix Potter was evidently thinking of the years to come when people might want to know more about her and about the

PLATE 8

'*She found some tiny canisters upon the dresser,
labelled—Rice—Coffee—Sago—but when she
turned them upside down, there was nothing
inside except red and blue beads*'

From *The Tale of Two Bad Mice*
by Beatrix Potter

Hill Top she loved. She was preparing the way by writing little notes containing information which were slipped in amongst her papers, attached to the backs of pictures hanging on the walls, and placed on other items of special interest. Similarly, at Castle Cottage, she had already sorted through her original drawings in their colourful hand-made portfolios adding, here and there, titles, dates and sundry remarks.

It was probably the effect of these cold, late, winter afternoons spent at Hill Top which hastened the attack of bronchitis from which Beatrix Potter died on 22nd December 1943, at the age of seventy-seven; but her work lives on, and will always be a source of delight to people of all ages and in all parts of the world.

A. L. LINDER

Title page illustration from
"The Tale of Tom Kitten"

Don Quixote and Sancho Panza

Drawing by Anthur Boyd Houghton

CHAPTER 8

The Present Company

PART I: 1919–1945

The new company, Frederick Warne & Company Limited, was duly registered on 25th May 1919 and the first board meeting was held on 30th June following, with Mr Harry Wingfield in the chair, the other directors present on the occasion being Mr C. F. Godfrey, Mr Arthur L. Stephens and Mr W. Fruing Warne. A year afterwards, on 25th August 1920, Mr Wingfield was officially appointed as Chairman and Mr Fruing Warne became the Managing Director. Of the hundred years of publishing which the house of Warne now celebrates, therefore, some fifty-five years were spent as a family business and partnership and the remainder as a limited company which continues with us today.

Among the early records of the new company were the sale of the film rights of Silas Hocking's *Her Benny* for the sum of £200—a modest figure by today's standards—and the signing of a contract with Emrik and Binger of Harlem for the production of a series of painting books. This firm, incidentally, afterwards printed and bound many series of what were then known as toy books, large flat books in colour with plenty of pictures and stiff paper covers. Sometimes these books were also printed on linen, with a stiffened cover.

Among the early publications of the new company was T. A. Coward's *Birds of the British Isles and their Eggs* to which we have previously referred. The first volume, published at 12*s*. 6*d*., appeared in February 1920, to be followed soon afterwards by the second volume which dealt mainly with sea-birds, while the third and final one on migrants and rare visitors was published in 1926. In 1924 Warne's acquired the right to include in these volumes reproductions from Lord Lilford's *Coloured Figures of British Birds* and these have proved an added feature to the work. All three volumes have had a steady sale over the years and are still in print, being revised and brought up-to-date as occasion demands. Coward's text, however, written in his own lucid style and with many personal touches which emphasize his own acute observation, is still basically unchanged.

Following on the formation of the limited company in London, the New York office was incorporated as a separate company on 4th June 1920 and in the December of that year Mr Arthur L. Treble left the London Export Department to take up duties and gain experience in New York, where he has since remained. We can recall his early observation that when in New York he was looked upon as an obvious Britisher and that whenever he visited England he was regarded as a goddarned Yankee. In those days he somehow felt that he was taking the knocks from both sides. As a younger man in London, by the way, Mr Treble had been a long-distance runner of distinction, having won several county championships and represented his country at the Olympic Games. On a more personal note still, of the five recorded instances over the past fifty years of a gentleman at Warne's first meeting his future wife as a fellow-employee, Mr Treble and the former Miss Locke are one such instance. Mr and Mrs Treble are now retired.

In October 1923, Mr Dick Billington, having left H.M. Stationery Office, joined the London Company as assistant to Mr W. A. Herring of the Production Department, where he remained an energetic worker for many years. He subsequently became a Director in 1940 and Managing Director in 1946, holding this latter position up to the time of his death in May 1960.

One activity which Mr Billington particularly concerned himself with during the 1920's and 1930's was the printing and production of many annuals, or bumper books as they were called, which the Company published at that time—Warne's Pleasure Books, Happy Books and Topall Books for boys, girls, children and toddlers respectively. These books were very much a feature of the period and were typical of the popular bulky type of annual publication produced by several publishers of children's books. Between bright covers, and for 2s. 6d., 2s. or 1s. 6d., according to title, young readers feasted on short stories, articles, poems and anecdotes, interspersed with a liberal

From "The Book of Nursery Tales",
drawing by H. M. Brock

supply of illustrations. As the years progressed and the competition among publishers became keener, some of these books grew almost to the size of family bibles. Although one still sees similar annual publications for children today, their bulk and variety are on a smaller scale than previously.

Within a few days of Mr Billington's joining the staff, Mr Frederick Warne Stephens, a grandson of the founder, was appointed to the Board in early November 1923. During this period of our history and for many years afterwards, Mr Stephens travelled annually to New Zealand, Australia and South Africa on the Company's behalf. It so happened that he was in New Zealand during the earthquake there in 1931, but fortunately was able to cable back home that he was safe and well.

The early days of the new Company coincided with a period of great social unrest in the country generally. Unemployment and strikes were a feature of the mid-1920's, culminating in the General Strike of 1926 which, as it happened, did not involve Warne's or its staff directly, although it naturally caused considerable inconvenience. A trade strike of the same era, however, did involve the warehouse staff in the only recorded strike that the firm has experienced, and when it was finally over, only a few "old faithfuls" were retained in the Company's employment.

Staff conditions generally were not unreasonable for the time and the Company's normal working day ended at 5.30 p.m. during the early months of the year and at 6.0 p.m. from mid-summer onwards as the volume of work increased, the pattern of trade being seasonal. Saturday work up to mid-day was also still the normal thing both at Warne's and elsewhere, but it became customary for the Company's staff to have one Saturday free in every month, thus getting a foretaste of the now accepted five-day week.

Soon after the First World War, office staff having more than ten years' service were allowed three weeks' annual holiday, and here we should like to recall Mr Charles Williams' first experience of this concession. When Mr Williams—then in the Counting House—thought he had fulfilled the necessary service requirement, he went to seek Mr Fruing Warne's official approval of his request for the extra holiday. Mr Fruing, who was busy at the time, promised to look into the matter at an early opportunity. Several weeks going by and Mr Williams hearing nothing further, he went again to Mr Fruing and asked if the latter "had looked into that little matter" which Mr Williams had queried. "Ah yes, my boy," said Mr Fruing Warne quickly, "we're giving you another £15 a year." Finding himself, to his surprise, with an increase in salary out of the blue, Mr Williams thought it best to defer his holiday request to a more opportune moment.

Another incident involving Mr Fruing Warne is an example of how the management may sometimes know more about its staff's ways than is supposed. Up to the mid-1920's there was no official afternoon tea-break at Warne's, but a number of the staff would slip away quietly to a back corner where a gas point enabled them to brew up tea in secrecy. One day Mr R. A. V. Priddle of the Binding Department was busy with Mr Warne over some stock figures when the latter looked at his watch and said, "Now then, run along and have your tea." Mr Priddle replied that the staff were not allowed any. "Go along," said Mr Fruing, "I know you all have it at the back of the third floor." So Mr Priddle departed, wondering how the hide-out had been discovered.

The 1920's, a period of change, also saw a social change whose effects today are now running at full flood. We refer to the arrival of the mass-produced motor car and its availability to the general public. Moving with the times, Warne's began in the mid-1920's to equip their travellers with motor cars and we understand that those early vintage models had quite a lot of rattle about them as soon as one reached top speed at 35–40 miles per hour. Before the advent of the motor car, travellers in the book trade had journeyed by train, and in big towns often employed a barrow-man to transport their samples from one customer to the next. Where the motor car eased the travellers' lot in this direction, the development of the book jacket, by this time coming into its own, tended to lighten his load in another, as a new book in a popular series could now be ordered by a bookseller on the sight of an attractive book jacket.

Regarding the Company's export sales to other English-speaking countries, we have already referred to Mr Fred Stephens' journeys to Australasia and South Africa and to the development of the New York Company. Hope for further success in this direction led to the appointment in December 1927 of Mr S. J. Reginald Saunders to represent the Company in Canada. Mr Saunders travelled with other companies' lines as well as Warne's list and his success led to the founding of his own company in Toronto, now one of the landmarks of the book trade in that country.

During the period that Mr Fruing Warne was Managing Director, the Company made slow but steady progress and continued to develop its popular-priced publications for children while still publishing an occasional new book from Beatrix Potter or Leslie Brooke. The back list of old favourites from earlier days was still a flourishing one and even Harrison Ainsworth's historical works had their place in the scheme of things beside the more general publications—dictionaries, letter-writers, cookery books and ready reckoners—which the Company had consistently produced and sold over the years. The Wayside and Woodland series was further extended by the publication of Edward Step's *Animal Life of the British Isles* (1921), *Life of The Wayside and Woodland* (1922) and B. Webster Smith's *World in the Past* (1926). The Company also continued to act as trade agents for Bartholomew's maps as it had been doing for many years previously.

From "The Book of Nursery Tales",
drawing by H. M. Brock

PLATE 9

From *Animals from Everywhere* by Clifford Webb

Mr W. Fruing Warne, partner of the old pre-war business and Managing Director of the new Company from its inception, died on 11th February 1928. Although he had been ill for some time, news of his death came rather unexpectedly to the staff, who mourned him as a friendly director and a charming person. He left a widow and family, but his son did not follow him into the business. As a matter of interest in view of the firm's many publications on entomology, Mr Fruing Warne in his time had been a great collector of butterflies.

In June 1928 came the appointment of Mr Arthur L. Stephens as the new Managing Director. He had already seen service as a director for some years and had combined this with the secretaryship of Messrs Spalding & Hodge, Ltd, the paper firm. Mr Stephens' son, Mr Cyril W. Stephens, was already on the staff of Warne's at this time and as a comparatively young man had done a certain amount of country travelling, before leaving for a five-year spell at the New York office, where he worked with Mr Treble.

In passing, it might be of interest to mention that about the time of Mr A. L. Stephens' appointment there were only three female members of the staff where today there are at least thirty. Of the three referred to, one was a secretarial-typist, another was receptionist and typist, while the third and junior was telephone- and post-girl plus typist. This last young lady entered every individual item of post in a book and answered the single line telephone, which was connected to a manual exchange before dialling was introduced to Covent Garden at the end of 1929. She still found time for some typing.

Among the publications of this period was the newly revised edition of Nuttall's *Dictionary*, edited by W. J. Gordon and others, which appeared in 1929 at a time when crossword puzzles were becoming extremely popular and word competitions abounded in magazines and newspapers. Puzzle compilers would often stipulate a well-known dictionary as the final arbiter on spelling and definition, and Nuttall's was often well to the fore in this connection.

In completely different vein the Company published English translations of several Italian monographs on famous painters, the books including copious illustrations in collotype. The first on *Michaelangelo* (1928) was perhaps as popular as any that followed. Afterwards came *Fra Angelico, Correggio, Pierro della Francesca* and *Sienese Painters of the Trecento*, in fairly rapid succession. All editions were finally sold, but there was not quite the same market for books of this type then that there might be today, now that colour photography and reproduction have helped to develop a public appreciation of books on the fine arts.

Books of a topographical nature had often found place in Warne's catalogue—*The Abbeys and Castles of England and Wales* and *The Romance of London* both being typical. A further move in this direction saw the publication of Halliwell Sutcliffe's *The Striding Dales* which described the dales, villages and people of Yorkshire. The book is still in print in a Crown 8vo format. The original 1929 edition was a handsome volume for the time and contained colour and line illustrations by A. Reginald Smith, R.W.S., who later also illustrated W. G. Collingwood's *The Lake Counties* (1932) in the same style. This latter book had a foreword by Hugh Walpole who had gone to live in the Lake District and who wrote glowingly of Collingwood's work. Then followed, over a period of a few years, a number of books with a Lakeland background—*The Secret Valley* and *Shelagh of Eskdale* by Nicholas Size, *Poems of Lakeland* compiled by Mrs Ashley P. Abraham, and finally *Hills of Lakeland* written and illustrated by W. Heaton Cooper, whose water colour drawings of Lakeland scenes are outstanding. Mr Heaton Cooper added *Tarns of Lakeland* and Mr B. L. Thompson added *Prose of Lakeland* to the list some years afterwards.

In 1930 Beatrix Potter, then over sixty, published her last Peter Rabbit Book—*The Tale of Little Pig Robinson*, with a text which was a fairly long one as compared with most of its predecessors. The book was first issued in a larger format but eventually came down to the well-known shape and size of its companions and became the twenty-third on the list. A few years afterwards, in 1935, Leslie Brooke's final *Johnny Crow's New Garden* appeared, similar in character to the previous Johnny Crow books, the author at the time being seventy-three.

In the field of natural history, during Mr Arthur Stephens' term as Managing Director, the Company added many notable

In Borrowdale

Drawing by A. Reginald Smith

titles to its already extensive list. *The Seas* by Drs Russell and Yonge first appeared during this time and the book has as recently as 1963 been revised by the same authors, the subject itself being now one of greater public interest than at possibly any time previously. *Bees, Wasps and Ants* by Edward Step, *Insects of the British Woodlands* by Dr Neil Chrystal and T. H. Savory's *Spiders and Allied Orders* all appeared in due course, while the more ambitious *Standard Natural History*, edited by W. P. Pycraft, appeared in 1936 and was a copiously illustrated 900 page-long survey of the whole of the animal kingdom. The Wayside Pocket Guides, which are shortened one-volume versions of larger Wayside and Woodland books, also made their appearance during the mid-1930's.

In yet another field were V. Wheeler-Holohan's editions of *Boutell's Heraldry* and *A Manual of Flags*. Mr Wheeler-Holohan was by profession a King's Messenger and he was also a heraldic artist of talent. His artwork was always meticulously finished and always reproduced well. Just before the Second World War one of his sons, Mr V. Wheeler-Holohan, Jr., joined Warne's staff. On the outbreak of hostilities this son was, as a member of the Territorial Army, called into service at an early date and unfortunately died abroad as a prisoner of war.

The foregoing books, many of which must have been costly ventures to produce, were published against a background of rising unemployment, the financial crisis in Great Britain, the Wall Street crash in America and the rise of Hitler to power in Europe. That the Company was sometimes pushed a little for ready cash and that it was unable at times to declare handsome dividends, can at least, on looking back, be seen as something perhaps excusable.

Yet within the firm itself there was a sense almost of patriarchal continuity at this time, as several members of the staff received presentations from their directors and colleagues either on the completion of fifty years' service with the Company or on retirement. Of Mr W. H. Greenwood we have already made mention, but another colleague, Mr T. E. ("Tommy") Webb of the Country Department, was presented with a gold watch in recognition of his work from 1883–1933. Mr Webb was on the stout side physically and had a gruff nononsense way with him which caused many a subordinate to quake when encountering his wrath. Underneath this exterior he was not unkindly, however, and during slack periods had been known to tell two or three of his men in his gruff undertone to "go and lose yourselves for an hour". He greatly enjoyed a glass of beer but it could never have harmed him as, retiring in 1938, he lived on to the ripe old age of ninety-two.

Other members of the staff who retired during the 1930's after many years of loyal service were: Mr Alfred ("Tosh") Brown, a warehouseman who quizzed at typematter through a pair of old pince-nez spectacles and walked with slow methodical tread; Mr W. ("Billy") Bambrick, a packer, who could not have been much over five feet tall in his socks and who had once been caretaker of the Bedford Street premises and, with Mrs Bambrick, had lived in the top floor rooms of No 15; finally Mr Jack Wood, the trade counter packer. Jack, a student of Dickens and Thackeray, was an interesting character who was spiritual brother to those grand old men behind the trade counter at Simpkins, the book wholesalers, in their Paternoster Row days. His other claims to fame were an unrivalled knowledge of the Company's out-of-print publications and the ability to eat a large spanish onion as nonchalantly as one might eat an apple. This particular feat, by the way, he performed daily for many years as a dessert to his lunch-time bread and cheese.

Mr T. H. Scott, the editor of this period, died in 1936. He was a quiet retiring personality, but in his more expansive moments had boasted of having in his time held down almost every journalistic job from gossip columns in a woman's magazine to the writing of adventure stories for boys, several of the latter, incidentally, being published by Warne's. He and Mr W. J. Stokoe, the Company's resident artist, were on friendly terms and lunched together. Mr Stokoe was a bearded and dignified gentleman who would descend the stairs at one o'clock and knock on Mr Scott's door and await his appearance. They would then solemnly walk off without, so far as one ever knew, a word being exchanged between them either coming or going.

Mr Stokoe retired in 1936 but had greatly interested himself in the Company's nature publications and from his retirement up to his death some years afterwards was generally busy compiling or editing one or other of the earlier Observer's books.

This series, the Observer's Pocket Series, was launched by the Company in 1938 and the first two titles to appear were *The Observer's Book of Birds* compiled by S. Vere Benson, and *The Observer's Book of Wild Flowers* compiled by W. J. Stokoe. By the

Early book jacket designs

time Mr Arthur Stephens retired in 1945, the series had grown to include ten titles with the main emphasis on nature subjects. The immediate post-war period, however, was to see the series expand sufficiently to include such subjects as architecture, ships and music. The series is still growing and the earlier titles are being constantly revised whenever need or opportunity arises.

One aspect of the Company's pre-war publishing programme was the growing interest shown in educational publishing. Mr Charles Williams, whom we have met earlier, was by this time the representative most concerned with exhibiting the firm's publications at educational conferences or calling on schools, and Warne's followed up these activities by publishing a number of reading books, and arts and crafts books mainly for school use. Mr Arthur Stephens and his advisers saw possibilities of expansion in this field and in post-war years the Company did in fact enlarge their educational list to a considerable degree.

Perhaps a word or two regarding Mr Arthur L. Stephens, the Company's Managing Director of this period, would not be amiss here. He was a quietly dressed and mild-mannered gentleman of the old school, who treated junior and senior alike with politeness and courtesy. As one who from circumstance became the managing director of a company with an established tradition and a staff who had served often many years within that tradition, he ruled with a glove rather than with an iron hand, but was respected by his staff nevertheless. A family man and a keen church-goer, he was not without a sense of humour. One amusing story concerning him is worth repeating. He was in conference with one or two senior staff on one occasion when another employee came in to complain about a colleague who had threatened to punch him on the nose following an argument. Mr Stephens promised to deal with the matter. It so happened that the person complaining was not the most popular member of the staff and as he closed the office door Mr Stephens with a smile turned to the others and said, "So X threatened to punch Y on the nose, did he? Then if he does, I'll give him a rise."

By 1939 the Company was beginning to develop and expand,

but the coming of the Second World War altered the whole picture. As the war progressed, many of the active male and female staff left the Company to serve in various capacities at home and overseas. At the same time, paper and print became scarcer as books were more sought after by the reading public as a form of recreation, readily available. Unfortunately as a result of enemy action alone, British publishers lost a total of twenty million books.

The Company suffered its own particular loss on the night of 29th December 1940 when all the sheet stock which had been transferred from the old warehouse at 13 Bucknall Street, W.C.2, to 47 Weston Street, S.E.1. was destroyed in an air raid. The end-of-the-year stocktaking had been completed and the stock sheets were to be seen hanging in a clip on the last wall left standing, before it, too, crashed into the rubble. On this same night, Paternoster Row, the very nerve centre of the London publishing trade, went up in flames with its stock of six million books.

Just prior to this disaster there had been some changes on the Company's Board of Directors which should be mentioned. Mr Cyril W. Stephens, son of Mr A. L. Stephens, was appointed a Director on 1st January 1940 while Mr Dick Billington and Mr W. A. Herring were elected to the Board in June 1940. Mr Herring was, with the exception of Mr F. W. Stephens, our longest serving member. Joining the firm in 1894, he was alleged to have retired in January 1946, but he worked on, partly at his Finchley home and partly at the office until the day before his death in October 1954.

In conjunction with these changes, Mr Harry Wingfield retired as Company Chairman in June 1940, having served the firm well in that capacity from 1919, and Mr C. F. Godfrey retired from the Board in the same month after a similar period of loyal service as a Director. Both died in 1944.

The war, terrible though it was, added its own flavour to everyday office life. At Warne's, for instance, an air-raid shelter was constructed in the basement, and after a lick of paint and a few pictures (from Warne's Chandos Jigsaw range) had been added to the walls and chairs and benches placed around for the staff's use, an otherwise humdrum area of basement was transformed into a moderately pleasant room. During the 1940's when sneak daylight raids were commonplace, the Company generally had a couple of roof-spotters and the staff worked on normally until a warning bell from the spotters advised them to go down to the basement.

During this period of the London blitz, one had no idea what buildings one might find had disappeared overnight, and the staff must often have gone home in the evening wondering whether Bedford Street would still be there the next day. Fortunately the street was not too badly affected, although a moderate hole was carved out of it near "Moss Bros" the outfitters and a time-bomb in Maiden Lane forced the firm to close its doors for a day or so. As time went on members of the staff were advised to leave the premises sufficiently early to enable them to be home during daylight and the hours of work were correspondingly shortened.

Of the younger staff who were called up under various forms of National Service, their jobs ranged from working in factories or joining the Land Army, to donning khaki or going to sea. Among these latter were Mr Rodney Fraser and Mr William Cappaert who as naval ratings met by chance in New York, both of them a long way from Bedford Street. Mr Fraser would also recount how he and his fellow shipmates were all sent to the U.S.A. to man a vessel which was being fitted out or repaired (we forget which) only to find that their future ship was still laid up. As time went by, Fraser and a fellow-rating were due for leave and asked the padre to advise where they could go. He eventually fixed them up with an address in a New England town and off they set by train. To their surprise a large crowd and a band was at their destination as the train pulled in and to their astonishment it was waiting for them. They were led off in a blaze of glory and next day banner headlines in the local newspaper read "British Tars hit Town".

On a more serious note, some members of the staff lost either home or personal effects as a result of bombing and two were wounded while serving overseas. Mr Charles Williams, while serving in the Air Force, had, with his comrades, to change ships in mid-ocean, their own one being hit.

Of the members of the staff who were killed while serving

overseas, mention has already been made of Mr V. Wheeler-Holohan, and with regret we must mention four others who did not return: Mr E. ("Ted") Auburn, who had worked as Mr Webb's assistant in the Country Department, Mr J. ("Jimmy") Marshall, who had also worked in that same department, Mr L. ("Joe") Eaves, who had served in various departments, and finally Mr W. ("Bill") Nettleton, who although not actually a member of the staff when he joined the Air Force, was nevertheless an old colleague known to many.

The end of World War II in the spring of 1945 found the Company in good shape in spite of paper restrictions. The firm's more popular titles were on a quota system during and just after the war so that booksellers obtained fair shares so far as stocks allowed. In September 1945 Warne's acquired the shares of R. J. Skinner Ltd (The Eden Press) from Messrs A. H. James & Co., and Mr F. W. Stephens became Chairman of this new company, with Mr D. Billington and Mr C. W. Stephens as his fellow Directors. The Eden Press is a general printers situated in premises just off Fleet Street (see p. 87).

At the end of 1945, Mr Arthur L. Stephens retired as Managing Director, after working with the Company over an eventful period of its history. He was still active, however, and was often calling in at the office as well as continuing to work at home. He lived on for another ten years and at the time of his death in July 1955 was over eighty.

Mr Dick Billington succeeded Mr Stephens as Managing Director on 1st January 1946. Mr Billington had served the Company as a Production Manager and Director over a number of years and he combined a sound technical knowledge with a keen interest in publishing and a desire to see the business develop and prosper now that the war was over. He was joined by Mr Cyril W. Stephens who became Company Secretary and an active full-time Director. Mr F. W. Stephens and Mr W. A. Herring, both of whom had served the firm over many years, continued to serve on the Board.

CHAPTER 9

The Present Company

PART II: 1945–1965

The years 1945–46 saw the return of the younger members of the staff who had been engaged in various war services and one of the problems naturally facing the newly formed Board was that of re-absorbing these people back into the business. That this was a problem was in part due to the unsettling influence of the time and the fact also that many of the staff had been away for anything up to five or six years, having gone out as juniors and returned as grown men.

Paper was still in short supply during the immediate post-war period and was allocated to publishers on a quota system, with the Directors and Production staff having to decide how best to make use of the supplies available. With stocks strictly limited in this way the Company was not too anxious to see its travellers back on the road, taking orders which might have little hope of being executed. Several of these men, feeling rather disheartened in the circumstances, finally accepted jobs with other publishers. As all of them had seen many years of service with the Company it was perhaps unfortunate that the problem had to be settled in this way. When more travellers were finally needed, younger men on the staff filled the empty places and are still there today.

Of those older travellers who remained, we should like to mention two. One is Mr Arthur King who followed Mr Barnard as Town traveller in 1944. Mr King joined the Company in 1912 as a traveller, then in the 1920's and 1930's was Export Manager and on the death of Mr Scott became Editor, and finally Town traveller, holding this last position until his retirement in 1963 after over fifty years with the Company. The other, Mr Harry Reding, was a Country traveller for many years before he retired from ill-health in 1952. He was, and still is, of a breezy, happy-go-lucky disposition and the fol-

From Summerhays' "Encyclopaedia for Horsemen",
drawing by John Board

lowing story of him would be typical. A South Wales customer
was once charged 9*s.* for some packing cases, for which he
consistently refused to pay and the Counting House finally
asked Mr Reding to try and get the matter settled one way
or the other when next in the South Wales area. In due course
Mr Reding surprisingly forwarded the customer's 9*s.* without
comment and he explained when he was next in the office how
he had got the money. It appeared that after some discussion
Mr Reding made the man a sporting offer to toss double or
quits for it. He agreed, they tossed and Mr Reding won. The
customer, his sporting instincts roused, suggested double or
quits in his turn, they tossed again and Mr Reding won a
second time, collecting 36*s.*, of which 9*s.* was duly sent on to
Bedford Street.

With Mr Billington appointed as Managing Director,
changes were necessary on the Production staff and Mr R. A. V.
Priddle, who had been Binding Department Manager for
many years, became Production Manager at this time.

With paper supplies to publishers then becoming more
readily available if used for educational purposes, the Company decided to develop this side of the catalogue with some
vigour and Mr Rodney Fraser, on leaving the Navy, joined the
Production Department on the educational side and remained
there a few years. School readers, textbooks for the very young,
nature books for schools, one-act playlets and assorted wall-
strips followed each other in profusion until the Company was
in a position to issue an independent Educational Catalogue.
With the volume of work thus developing, Mr A. F. Stuart
became Art Editor after several years in the Art Department
following on Mr Stokoe's retirement.

Mr Billington's son, Richard, joined the staff in 1947, and after a short period at the London office was transferred to the New York Company, where he has since remained. He tells us that he is now very much at home over there. He was, incidentally, preceded by a young lady on the London staff, Miss Audrey Bailey, who spent two years at the New York office before returning once more, complete with both an attractive accent and an attractive wardrobe, to a London of austerity and "utility" clothing.

There were considerable changes in the packing and warehouse staff during this post-war period. Many of the newcomers who joined us then as replacements are still with us, however, in this centenary year and have almost now become "old-stagers" in their turn. We should like here to recall one genuine "old-stager", Mr R. ("Bob") Lyons, a packer who died in 1951 in harness, having joined the Company in 1911. His nephew, Mr S. Hughes, is now in 1965 the Foreman Packer.

Three other changes behind the scenes in the period under review were the installation of a new internal telephone system, the mechanization of the Counting House, then jointly managed by Mr S. R. Smith and Mr C. Masterton, Mr Arthur Emery having retired in 1945, and the addition of an extra floor to the Bedford Court premises.

Regarding the internal telephone system, still in use (which replaced a veritable "Heath Robinson" apparatus that older staff members will recall), it was so arranged that the line from the Director's office can always cut in on any other line in use, and two members of the staff once mutually complaining about Mr Billington and what they thought of the "Old Man's" instructions on a particular issue, were suddenly startled to hear a well-known voice say "Never mind what you think the Old Man should do, you just do what the Old Man tells you!"

In respect of the mechanization of the Counting House and the consequent employment of young lady accounting-machine operators, this brought to an end the rather unique contribution that department had made to the Company's history over the years. Just for the record we list ex-Counting House members who began as ledger clerks and who subsequently developed further or elsewhere:

T. C. Opher	1898	Suburban traveller to 1944
A. Emery	1899	Cashier 1911–45
F. Moss	1917	Trade Counter Manager & Traveller
C. S. Williams	1919	Traveller 1930–1947
F. Armstrong	1927	Production Staff
A. F. Stuart	1929	Art Editor 1949
S. R. Smith	1930	Company Secretary 1960
R. E. Weir	1939	Traveller 1948
W. Butcher	1939	Traveller
J. F. Heard	1940	Export Manager 1945

In the above list, the date following the surname shows the year each man started work in the Counting House and the right-hand column his approximate later career with the Company.

The extra top floor was added to the Bedford Court premises in 1950 and the Production and Editorial Departments were moved into the new office space then made available. The remainder of the new floor space was fitted out as a staff canteen which has proved a boon to the staff generally by providing daily meals and snacks at nominal charges. The opportunity was also taken at this time to install a passenger lift giving access to all floors.

In August 1951 the Newdigate Press, a small bindery, was purchased by the Company from Messrs King & Jarrett. It was then trading from the village of Newdigate, a few miles south of Dorking in Surrey, and the premises at that time comprised some three Nissen huts and remained so until 1954 when a move was made to Dorking. Here new factory premises were built, and under the guidance of the Manager, Mr N. F. Martyr, the works have continued to grow and the Company to prosper. Further details regarding this venture will be found on p. 87.

Among the general publications of this time were several additions to the ever-popular Observer's books, notably *Horses and Ponies* by R. S. Summerhays, *Aircraft* by Green and Pollinger and *Architecture* by Ryan and Penoyre. Mr Green's efforts on behalf of the *Observer's Book of Aircraft* have been outstanding and a new edition of the book has appeared annually for many years now, the title proving to be one of the most successful in the series. Mr Summerhays, who has been known as a horse-man and show judge of note over a long period, eventually compiled *Summerhays' Encyclopaedia for Horsemen* which Warne's published in 1952 and both this book and the Observer's Book have been through several editions. Messrs Ryan and Penoyre's small book on *Architecture* has always been warmly praised and is a remarkable instance of how to get a quart into a pint pot. This title has also been revised and reprinted several times.

Drawing from the "Observer's Book of Architecture"

A complete revision of Nuttall's *Dictionary* was undertaken at this time by H. Lawrence Dawson and the new edition of 1951 was completely restyled and reset in conformity with present-day needs and tastes. Although the book now has many rivals in its field, we are glad to say that this centenarian among popular-priced dictionaries still holds its place in the catalogue. The Nuttall *Encyclopaedia*, its companion volume, received a similar overhaul in 1956 and also maintains its place as a handy one-volume reference book.

On the juvenile side of the catalogue, the Company issued a revised version of Clifford Webb's *Story of Noah* with the author contributing a new centre colour section. Mr Webb and his wife, who uses the pen-name of Ella Monckton, have, singly and together, added many titles to Warne's list and Mr Webb's work is particularly referred to on p. 100.

Among other illustrated books for children of this period were the additional titles to the Jane Tompkins series of animal

*From "The Story of Mr Prettimouse",
illustrated by Mary B. Robinson*

books—*The Polar Bear Twins, Red Squirrel Twins, Reindeer Twins,*
etc.; *Bible Stories for Children* by Gladys Taylor, with pictures
by Paul Dessau (also issued as individual stories); *Johann the
Woodcarver* by Gilmore Wood, with pictures by Margaret
Tarrant; and *The Little Good People* a collection of Irish fairy
stories by Kathleen Foyle, with illustrations by Peter Fraser.

Two series of books for the very young were started at this
time: The Prettimouse Series of illustrated stories concerning
various animals and their adventures, and The Teddy Bear
Coalman Series intended as simple picture and story books for
the three- to six-year-olds. All of these books are still in print and
extra titles to the series have been added from time to time.

The work of Beatrix Potter was not overlooked (she had
died in 1942) and Margaret Lane's successful biography *The
Tale of Beatrix Potter* (1946) brought to public notice for the
first time Miss Potter's strict Victorian upbringing and her
early attempts to publish her work and establish her own independence in life. The book continued with the story of her
eventual marriage and later career as a Lake District sheep
farmer. In 1952 an English edition of *The Fairy Caravan* was
issued by the London house, the book having previously been
published by David McKay of Philadelphia. Miss Potter wrote
the story for older children and the book is illustrated with
colour plates and line drawings by its author.

Finally in 1955 came *The Art of Beatrix Potter,* a handsome volume compiled by L. Linder and W. A. Herring, which did full justice to her work as an artist in many fields. When Mr Linder, himself a keen collector of her work, suggested such a book to the Company, there was some initial hesitation about it, so he tells us, but once the idea was accepted, the work was taken up with great interest. Mr Herring, at that time a Director of the Company and one who had known Miss Potter in former years, assisted in the choice of illustration and brought the work through many of the earlier stages of production. He unfortunately died before its final publication and Mr R. A. V. Priddle saw it through the press, making journeys to the colour printers to ascertain that all was well. The book gave her many admirers an opportunity to keep a permanent record of her work both as the creator of a whole gallery of nursery characters and as a water-colourist of distinction.

New revised editions both of *Boutell's Heraldry* and *Flags of the World* were commissioned, and the Company were fortunate in obtaining the services of two outstanding authorities on both subjects—Mr G. W. Scott-Giles for *Boutell* and Mr H. Gresham Carr for *Flags.* Mr Scott-Giles' work in the field of heraldry was acknowledged when he eventually received the honorary title of Fitzalan Pursuivant of Arms Extraordinary, and Mr Gresham Carr was also an enthusiastic expert on his subject and a friendly personality.

Mr Carr once told us how he was invited to give a flag lecture to a group of young London cockney lads. He arrived on the lecture platform with his notes and a box of flags, both parties eyeing each other somewhat warily, when a voice from the audience called out "Bet you 'aven't got the skull'n crossbones flag there, guvnor!" Mr Carr, who knew both his homework and his Londoners, without a word produced it immediately from his box, leaving his young audience impressed and speechless. The Company heard of his death in 1962 with regret.

There were several important additions to the Wayside and Woodland series during the first ten years after the war, with such books as Colyer and Hammond's *Flies of the British Isles* (1951), John Clegg's *Freshwater Life of the British Isles* (1952), followed by E. F. Linssen's *Beetles of the British Isles* (2 vols., 1959), and somewhat later, Southwood and Leston's *Land and Water Bugs of the British Isles* (1959).

During the whole period of Mr Billington's term as Managing Director the Observer's series continued to grow, until by the late 1950's there were practically thirty titles in the series on topics far removed from the earlier nature subjects, although the latter side was never forgotten, as *Garden Flowers*, *Cacti* and *Sea Fishes*, for instance, will testify. Such popular titles as *Automobiles* and *Railway Locomotives*, however, have an obvious appeal to the older schoolboy and they sell in their thousands annually, while the *Observer's Book of Music* by Freda Dinn and the *Observer's Book of Painting and Graphic Art* by William Gaunt cater for the more adult reader. We have, by the way, always admired Mr Gaunt's book for its conciseness and balanced viewpoint, and both this book and his more recent *Observer's Book of Modern Art* are one-third the price of any similar survey on the same subjects, apart from possible paperback titles.

An unusual book which was well in production during 1959 or so (but did not finally appear until 1961) was John Bromley's *Armorial Bearings of the Guilds of London* with forty colour plates by Heather Child. The book had first been suggested as a semi-private venture for sale among members of the fifty city Companies and their friends and associates, but Warne's took the opportunity to print a normal trade edition at the same time. Miss Heather Child's colour plates are particularly attractive and the originals were painted on vellum to form a permanent heraldic record for subsequent display as required.

During the 1950's the Company published several illustrated books for children by two fine animal artists—K. Nixon and Inga Borg. Miss Nixon is particularly interested in the domesticated cat and dog as well as wild animals generally, while Miss Borg is more concerned with the lives of those animals of her native Sweden. Miss Borg's books are simultaneously published in Swedish and Warne's have acquired the English language rights. Some further remarks on both artists can be found on pp. 103 and 104.

Returning once more to business issues, the firm continued

to increase its sales and enlarge its interests up to the time of Mr Billington's death in 1960. Whereas in pre-war days the trade had been largely a seasonal one, with the first three months of the year as an extremely quiet trading period, the post-war tendency has been to see this period as a far more busy time than previously, with the volume of work increasing as the year progresses.

In 1958 Warne's increased its share capital and around this time began to develop the premises at Dorking to include warehouse space for the parent company. With a publishing list such as Warne's has, where a book may have a normal life covering a span of years, every additional title means an extra stock-bin and extra storage space of some sort. In a list of 600–700 individually catalogued items this can understandably be quite a problem. Editions today tend to run to larger numbers than in former years, partly as a result of increased turnover and also in an attempt to reduce costs, and where the whole edition is unlikely to be bound up in one fell swoop, there will naturally be flat sheet stock to be stored for future use.

In 1958 the Company lost one of its older servants Mr F. ("Algy") Eldridge, who had been Warne's van driver in the pre-1914 era of horses and carts and who continued in a later and more mechanized day to serve both the Company and its customers with equal loyalty. The nature of his calling led him into many adventures and we shall mention one. Being asked once to transport one of the senior staff to a given address and fearing that this might create a precedent, he drove with assumed carelessness (as he afterwards privately confessed), cursed or threatened to fight all and sundry that got anywhere near him on the road and finally dropped a passenger only too relieved to get out after having sat most of the time with his eyes shut. This particular gentleman, by the way, never asked for a second lift. If Algy had to report a minor accident to his superiors, he would describe the incident in his own particular cockney idiom, which would then be transformed into an impeccable prose statement ("I was proceeding in a westerly direction towards Knightsbridge . . . etc.") which he would then sign as a true account of the facts. Somehow, however, we always preferred his own salty version.

Drawing by V. Wheeler-Holohan for "Boutell's Heraldry"
(above) and by Heather Child for "Armorial Bearings of the
Guilds of London"

Mr Billington, after thirty-six years with the Company and with fourteen years service as Managing Director, died suddenly in the late spring of 1960. Although he had spent many years working in London, he had always been a countryman at heart, and in the 1920's and 1930's when many of the staff lived in such London suburbs as Acton, Clapham or Highgate, he had commuted daily from Hemel Hempstead in Hertfordshire, while in later years he lived in Surrey. He had a good tenor voice, was a keen admirer of the Gilbert and Sullivan operas and had been a founder-member of the Book Trade Operatic and Dramatic Society which flourished in the early 1930's. He could be quick of temper in the office whenever he thought things had gone awry, but once the fires died down he soon became his usual self. He was one of those people who are known by their initials—among the staff at Warne's he was almost always D.B.

The present Managing Director, Mr Cyril W. Stephens, was appointed on the 3rd May 1960 and Mr R. A. V. Priddle and Mr S. R. Smith joined the Board at this time. Mr Stephens had been active in the business for many years both as Company Secretary and as Mr Billington's right-hand man and the choice was therefore an obvious one. At the end of 1964 Mr F. W. Stephens retired from the Company Chairmanship and was succeeded by Mr Cyril Stephens, who now holds the combined position of Chairman and Managing Director. Mr R. A. V. Priddle, having joined the Company as a young man in 1917 and served in the Binding Department under Mr Harry Messenger, was later made Binding Manager and then Production Manager before joining the Board. Mr S. R. Smith, the new Company Secretary, had been the Counting House senior clerk under Mr A. Emery from 1930 onwards and had assumed a more responsible position in the department during the postwar period. Mr L. Morgan, who had joined the Production staff in 1956, became the new Production Manager following on Mr Priddle's appointment.

The publishing programme of the new Board continued to follow the same general trends of previous years. In mentioning this, it must of course be borne in mind that a publisher's future plans are always anything between six months and two years

From "He Looks this Way"
by Cécile Curtis

ahead of publication and that a certain amount of back-log is inevitable in any circumstances involving change.

Even so, however, the Company has only modified its policy where changing tastes in reading may seem to require it. There is a preference, for instance, with regard to books for older children today, for those which are instructional and informative, rather than for purely fictional ones, and Warne's have followed this trend in recent years.

Such books for boys as those on *Electricity*, *Power Stations* and *Water Power* by Geoffrey Gerard, *Inventors of the World* and

G

Engineers of the World by I. O. Evans, together with the titles in the Young Scientist series, are all in this category, while similar books for girls are *Women Who Made History* by Mary Cathcart Borer and *The Book of Ballet* by James Audsley.

For younger children, the Company has tended to wait for what it considers an interesting story or idea and illustrate and produce it as well as the price-range will allow, rather than attempt competing with the cheaper mass-produced picture book of today, this latter article being very much the product of the larger publishing companies who are especially concerned with turnover and large printing runs. In this respect, Warne's, as an old-established medium-sized house, has not the financial or technical resources for such ventures and must trim its sails accordingly.

The Company has continued to publish new books by Clifford Webb, K. Nixon and Inga Borg for younger children and has also commenced a new series of Little Folks' Books— Nursery Rhymes, Nursery Tales, and First and Second Books— with charming illustrations by Rene Cloke. Dorothy Whipple's two stories about tortoises and Jean Marshall's Little Story Books, all illustrated by Hubert Williams, are also intended for younger readers. A further new venture is Cécile Curtis's *He Looks This Way*, with attractive illustrations in scraperboard.

In the Observer's series, Patrick Moore's *Astronomy*, William Gaunt's *Modern Art* and John Woodford's *Furniture* are all first-rate additions to a series which now reaches a total of over thirty-five volumes. The Company are naturally not only actively considering further additions to this series but are always taking care to keep older titles up-to-date in subject-matter and presentation.

With regard to the Wayside and Woodland series, several of the standard titles have been extensively revised in recent years. South's *Moths of the British Isles* for instance has been revised by H. M. Edelsten, with a completely new set of colour plates by the late H. D. Swain, F.R.E.S.; Step's former *Life of the Wayside and Woodland* has been re-written by Dr T. R. E. Southwood and re-illustrated throughout; and *Wayside and Woodland Trees* has been thoroughly revised by Herbert Edlin

Drawing from the "Encyclopaedia of Southern Africa"

of the Forestry Commission. Russell and Yonge's *The Seas* and Step's *Wayside and Woodland Blossoms* have also been revised over the past year or two, while R. L. E. Ford, F.R.E.S., has added a new volume to the series on *Practical Entomology*. The Company now has Mr John Clegg, author and naturalist, as its editorial adviser on nature publications generally.

Concerning the firm's more general publications, *Boutell's Heraldry* and *The Encyclopaedia of Southern Africa* have both been revised and re-issued in recent times, while the list of books on hobbies and handicrafts has been considerably augmented.

It will therefore be seen that in the five short years since the new Board was appointed, the Company has made every effort to continue the production momentum of previous years and develop and expand the business wherever possible. On the practical side, further building extensions at Dorking have greatly increased the warehouse space now available and considerable stocks are now held in these new premises. On the staff side, Warne's still retains, as in previous generations, a hard core of loyal staff members who have served the Company over a long period of years and have helped to preserve that sense of continuity with the past which the celebration of a centenary would naturally imply.

We therefore bring to a close this review of the progress of the house of Warne over the past century: from 1865, when even royalty went to bed by candle-light, to 1965, when men only have to press a switch and a rocket will travel to the moon. Over the whole of the intervening years of tremendous change —political, social and economic—a man might have walked into a bookshop in almost any part of the world and come away with a Warne book tucked under his arm. The Company hopes he will still be able to do so for a very long time.

The following is a list of present staff who have served 25 years or more with the firm:

Frederick Warne Stephens	J. Felstead
Cyril W. Stephens	J. Heard
R. A. V. Priddle	S. Hughes
S. R. Smith	Miss Alice Stone
W. Bagshaw	A. F. Stuart
C. Butler	R. E. Weir
G. Cappaert	

We give here a brief note, in case it may be of interest, on Warne's colophon, the wings and horseshoe device sometimes seen on our publications.

It was first used by the Company in Victorian times and the early printed versions of the design showed the ends of the horseshoe pointing downwards with the torse or twisted ribbon placed as a straight horizontal band beneath the wings.

Following on the re-issue of *Boutell's Heraldry* in 1931, the Company sought advice regarding the heraldic basis of the design, which was understood to have been connected at one time with a branch of the Warne family. It was then decided, as being more correct, to turn the horseshoe the other way so that the points were uppermost and at the same time to re-design the wings and torse. This revised version of the colophon has been used by the Company from that time.

CHAPTER 10

The Eden Press and The Newdigate Press

It was in 1945 that Warne's decided to branch out a little. Messrs A. H. James owned the shares in a small printing business and in September of that year these shares were transferred to Frederick Warne & Co. Ltd. The business was only a small one, situated in Eden Street, from whence it got its name. Soon after the takeover the business was transferred to a basement at Wheatsheaf House in Carmelite Street, E.C.4. It had a small staff led by Mr Newsom, and much of its work consisted of printing leaflets and book jackets for Frederick Warne.

Mr Newsom was a kindly man, who always liked to wear a buttonhole picked from his own garden. If ever he had to appear without it he was most upset. Ill health forced him to retire in 1956, and a new manager was installed. Unfortunately he left after a short while, and Mr C. Green took over the job of management. He is still in charge, having been made a Director of Eden Press in July 1962.

The firm is still in the same basement premises, but under Mr Green's guidance it has been able to expand and install more modern machinery, thus enabling it to tackle more advanced work, especially in the field of colour and book printing. It still does a fair amount of work for Warne's but it has many other customers mostly in and around London.

The Newdigate Press was originally a small bindery owned by Messrs King and Jarrett and was situated in the village of Newdigate some five miles south of Dorking in Surrey.

It had been doing a certain amount of handfolding on Leslie Brooke sheets for Warne's for shipment to the New York house —work which at the time other binders had been unable to undertake—when it became known that King and Jarrett were about to close down the bindery.

After considering the matter, Warne's decided to purchase the business and finally took control on 9th August 1951.

The Newdigate Press at this time was housed in three Nissen huts, each thirty yards apart, employing a small but loyal staff under the direction of Mr N. F. Martyr, all of them keen to put the business on the map.

Warne's were equally keen to see their new venture succeed and eventually a site was acquired in Vincent Lane, Dorking, where a new factory could be built. Work was put in hand and the Newdigate Press duly installed on 28th July 1954, the staff at this time being thirteen men and fourteen girls.

During a lunch to celebrate the occasion and held in Dorking, the then Chairman, Mr F. W. Stephens, spoke of the kind of work it was hoped the factory might one day undertake, especially in the field of special bindings for export to countries with particular climatic conditions, a hope, by the way, which has since been realized.

The story of the Newdigate Press since those early days has been one of consistent progress and growth. In October 1956 a new warehouse was erected to cope with the Company's increasing output and the number of staff gradually increased as new or more up-to-date machinery was installed when circumstances permitted. In June 1958 a further warehouse was completed at Dorking, with the addition of a basement warehouse for Warne's, while at the same time the factory space was enlarged and production again increased. Then in 1960 further building extensions gave additional space to both the factory and Warne's basement warehouse, while finally in 1964 a three-storey office block was added to form a completely new frontage to the earlier premises. The Newdigate Press has now moved office into the ground floor of this new block to allow their former office space to be used as factory extension, thus bringing the story more or less up-to-date.

While a certain proportion of Newdigate's binding work has naturally come from Warne's, the Managing Director, Mr N. F. Martyr, has made every effort to enlarge the scope of the business and work is now completed for many other publishers.

Today the factory is a pleasant airy building on ground floor level, where some thirty-five men and forty-odd women are employed, and where each binding stage follows on progressively from one section of the floor to the next. Stacks of sheet stock, or books in varying stages of completion are ranged at strategic spots, while the factory machines fold, collate, sew and stitch until the guillotine makes each copy neat and tidy enough to receive its binding case and finally its book jacket, with packing and dispatch as the ultimate link in the chain.

While all this goes on inside the factory, outside in the Surrey air one can see the North Downs above Ranmore, and in the distance, the vantage-point of Box Hill, while nearer still is the slender spire of Dorking church and the red roofs of the town itself. In spite of the buses and the traffic, Bedford Street and the Strand and London's thriving millions seem somehow a long way off.

"The Milkmaid",
drawing by Randolph Caldecott

CHAPTER II

Overseas Representatives

Shortly after the Second World War Warne's were approached by a person who shall be nameless to represent them in an overseas territory. In company with other publishers they supplied him with samples and money. They wished him "good luck" and that was the last they ever heard of him!

Apart from this experience Warne's have been very fortunate in their choice of representatives and on the following pages will be found some account of the various companies and persons who have been and are still selling the Company's publications in nearly every corner of the world.

S. J. Reginald Saunders & Co. Ltd.   Toronto.

The Saunders Company of Canada was established by the late Reggie Saunders, an ex-Blue Coat Schoolboy in England, who, following a spell with the Artillery in the First World War, joined the firm of Sandle Brothers and Company of London and became their Export Manager. In this position he decided to tackle the Canadian market and made several trips to Canada before finally opening an office on his own account in 1933 as the representative of several publishing companies including Frederick Warne. His original stocks were sent to him on a consignment basis, which in a sense gave him some capital to develop the business.

He was a most unusual character and was beloved by the trade from coast to coast. He married a Canadian girl, but the couple had no family and on his death in 1945 his widow and her fellow trustees looked for somebody to manage the business and Mr Victor Knight joined the Company in this capacity.

Like his predecessor, Mr Knight was born in England—in fact he claims that he was born within the sound of Bow Bells when the wind was in the right quarter—and the Knight family migrated to Canada in 1913. As a young man, Victor's first venture into the commercial world was not a success. The year 1919 saw him helping to develop prints and edit film in a motion picture company, but he soon realized that all was not well and after six months of it he decided to leave. As two members of the company later served prison sentences, it was perhaps just as well.

At the age of eighteen, Victor joined his father's Christmas card business and his assignment of selling cards from Toronto to Vancouver on a door-to-door basis and later to retail stores, gave him valuable experience and no doubt a wide geographical knowledge of his new country.

After undertaking various business assignments, he became in 1938 the Advertising Manager of W. J. Gage & Co., with whom he served until 1945, when he joined the Saunders Company as Manager for the estate. Nine years later, in partnership with Mr Ross McDonald, who had been with the Company for many years, and with the help of his friend F. D. Allen, the business was purchased with Victor Knight acting as Managing Director.

During his time with the Saunders Company Victor Knight has served in various capacities in connection with the Book Publishers' Association of Canada and was at one time its President. Currently he is Chairman of the Customs and Transportation Committee of the Canadian Book Publishers' Council and also the English Vice-President (there is also a French-Canadian Vice-President) of Canadian Library Week which supports a National Book Week.

It was during the early days of the formation of the Young Canada's Book Week, in fact at the first meeting of the children's librarians in this connection, that Victor Knight found himself as the only man present at a luncheon of some seventy-five librarians and the main speaker commenced by saying "Madam Chairman, Ladies, and Peter Rabbit". The name has stuck and Victor frequently gets letters addressed to "Dear Peter". Mrs Knight, incidentally, shares her husband's love of books, and she is divisional head of the Children's Department of the North York Public Library system, adjacent to Toronto. Both of them are also keen and active members of the Unitarian Church.

The Saunders Company today occupies about 14,000 square feet of warehouse and office space, has a staff of twenty-two people, and is doing a turnover in books alone which is over five times as great as that of 1945, the year of Mr Saunders' death. Most of the important agencies have been retained, although the Company has dropped out of the stationery business completely. The business continues to prosper and is a household name in the Canadian book trade.

J. R. & D. L. Dorman.   Johannesburg, S. Africa.

Up to the beginning of the Second World War, South Africa was visited annually by Mr Frederick Warne Stephens, and he usually called at various cities of the Union, including Johannesburg.

After the war, Mr Stephens retired from his previous active occupation and it was not until 1955 that Mr Albert Watson was appointed as Warne's representative in the area, which at the time also covered the Rhodesias and Nyasaland. It was due to the enthusiasm of Mr Watson that Warne's eventually published, in 1961, the *Encyclopaedia of Southern Africa* edited by Eric Rosenthal, as well as two *Rand-Cent Ready Reckoners* to meet South Africa's change over to decimal coinage.

Mr Albert Watson returned to Great Britain in 1961 and in the same year J. R. & D. L. Dorman, at that time of Durban, became Warne's representatives for South Africa.

John Dorman started "on the road" in South Africa in 1933, being then twenty-four years of age, and carried the samples of Raphael Tuck & Sons Ltd. Later that same year he commenced representing his first book publisher, The Religious Tract Society, now known as the Lutterworth Press, and by 1938 he had also come to represent both J. M. Dent & Sons, Ltd, and the Cambridge University Press, still today being happily associated with all of them. Married, with one son, he was once a keen tennis player and golfer, but his main activity now is gardening.

In 1948, his brother Dennis joined the business, having previously served in North Africa during the Second World War, becoming eventually a prisoner of war in Germany. He is also married, with two children and enjoys a game of bowls.

In 1958 the Dormans moved from Durban to Johannesburg, as being the largest city in a more central position, with the added advantage of having a better climate.

Allied Publishers Private Limited. Bombay and branches, India.

In 1934, Mr M. Graham Brash founded the Allied Publishers and Stationery Manufacturers Ltd (as it was then known) with offices in Bombay, and at the same time commenced to act as Frederick Warne's agents in India. Mr Graham Brash, a shrewd and hardworking business man, became highly respected in the Indian book trade and by 1938 had opened a branch office in Calcutta. The outbreak of war in 1939 found the Company firmly established.

During the Second World War, book stocks became insufficient for the growing needs of both the civilian population and the armed forces stationed in India, and booksellers would on occasions sit on the Allied Publishers' doorstep awaiting the release of books by the Post Office. Sometimes they were even prepared to take the complete contents of parcels without wanting to know the titles of the books inside, so great was the demand.

With the aftermath of war and the stress and strain following upon Independence, Mr Graham Brash thought it advisable in 1947 to relinquish control of the Company to Mr R. N. Sachdev and Mr P. C. Manaktala, although he continued to act as Managing Director until 1954, when he left the Company to start a new business in Hong Kong, which, incidentally, is now managed by his son.

Mr Manaktala succeeded Mr Brash as Managing Director and with new branches opened at Delhi in 1952, and at Madras in 1961, the business has now grown to some twenty times the volume of trade of 1947. Allied Publishers claim that there is hardly a subject, age-group or level of scholarship for which they are unable to supply the relevant books.

The Chairman, Mr Sachdev, has shown great vision in helping to expand the company's activities, while Mr Manaktala, with a fine academic career behind him, continues to act as Managing Director. Mr Manaktala, who is a keen amateur photographer, was founder President of the Leica Club of India.

He has also held many offices of distinction in the various book trade organizations of India.

Allied Publishers is well served by the managers and staff of its various branches, and both Mr A. N. Srinivas (Secretary) and Mr B. K. Achar (Bombay Manager) have been in the business from Mr Brash's earliest days of over thirty years ago.

Donald Moore Ltd.   Singapore, Hong Kong, Tokio etc.

The Donald Moore organization began to develop in the Far East soon after the end of the Second World War, when Donald Moore, having quitted the lower deck of the British Navy (his university, so he tells us) and his final position in the senior service as Lieutenant R.N.V.R., became a publisher's representative. This was in 1947, and by 1955 he began to publish on his own account, being himself an author of some ten books— fiction, children's books, thrillers and anthologies—published mainly in Great Britain.

Donald Moore Ltd opened their first bookshop in 1962, and today they have branches in many Far Eastern cities, with the main ones in Singapore, Hong Kong and Tokio. They have represented Frederick Warne in the area since 1959 and now look after the interests of a great many British publishers in the Far East.

Donald Moore, the founder of all this activity, is now a married man with four children (perhaps five, he trusts, by the time we go to press), and his ambition, surprisingly enough, is to retire to a vast and powerful motorized caravan, thereafter to trundle joyously round Europe, of which he knows so little. The staff of Frederick Warne and Company, urged by vast travel agencies and airline networks to visit, funds permitting, the glamorous East, realize that each man has his own Shangri-La.

Joyce Lindrea Ltd.   Salisbury, Rhodesia.

Joyce Lindrea, who became Warne's representative in January 1961 in the Rhodesias (including the present Zambia) and Nyasaland (now Malawi), began her literary career delivering newspapers in the delightful English village of Nether Stowey in Somerset.

Having risen from this humble beginning to the dizzy heights, as she puts it, of being a publishers' representative, she has had her share of adventures in Central Africa. She recalls, on one occasion, her car being stoned by thugs, and on another, of having to meet an African headmaster by appointment, only to find that under the influence of the local witch-doctor he had reverted to type and was capering around in a leopard skin.

Her adventures, by the way, are shared with an Alsatian dog, who must, one imagines, be a useful companion-help at times. She is also not without her traffic problems, but instead of traffic jams she is held up by herds of elephant. We have no knowledge of what Nether Stowey folk would think of it all, but presumably for Joyce Lindrea it is all part of a day's work.

Dr H. R. Conrad.   Meilen, Switzerland.

Born at Muswell Hill in North London in 1912, Dr H. R. Conrad began his first continental travels at the tender age of nine months, his parents being of French–Swiss nationality.

He was educated at King's College, Cambridge, where he gained a Ph.D. and showed prowess as a tennis player by winning a bronze medal at the Middlesex Junior Championships and Fenner's colours at Cambridge. Rock climbing is one of his present-day pastimes, and in company with his wife he has climbed such famous Alpine peaks as the Eiger and the Wetterhorn. Dr Conrad and his wife are also both keen travellers, while other activities include long-distance motoring, and knowing about wine and drinking some.

It was in 1949 that he commenced to represent Warne's, showing the Company's publications to bookshops in Switzerland, West Germany and Luxembourg. His difficulties in selling English books can be gauged by the fact that in the whole of his territory there are only two bookshops actually stocking English books, with a further fifteen having what may be called an English department.

Among other firms he also represents the powerful Heinemann group of publishers and is a familiar figure at their stand at the famous Frankfurt Book Fair.

C. L. Walker.   West Indies.

In 1963, after a period of some twenty-two years in the

Colonial Service, Mr C. L. Walker decided on a new career—
that of selling books in the West Indies, with headquarters at
Bridgetown, Barbados. He was no stranger to the area, having
family and business connections there, and he has since travelled
widely throughout the Islands as a publishers' representative.
He numbers Frederick Warne and Company among the small
group of firms he represents.

Hicks, Smith & Sons Pty, Ltd.   Australia and New Zealand.

Hicks, Smith & Wright, as the company was called until
1951, have been in business for many years in the Southern
Hemisphere, having represented English publishers since 1912
and Frederick Warne in particular since the 1920's. The original
business partners were Mr G. J. Hicks, who died in 1953, and
Mr W. Smith, a still hale and hearty Chairman of Directors for
the three companies which today make up the Hicks Smith
group.

Some older staff members of earlier days can recall Mr
Frederick Warne Stephens' annual visit, when he left England
in November to arrive at Dunedin, New Zealand, in Christmas
week. As this particular city was his farthest call from London,
Mr Stephens would tell his clients that from then onwards he
was starting on his way home, even though he still had Australia
and South Africa to visit.

Before the mid-1920's the firm's headquarters were in Wellington, New Zealand, and the partners would visit Australia each
year. In 1923 Mr J. A. Hicks (son of G. J. Hicks) went to
Melbourne and opened up the company's Australian branch.
Then in 1926 Mr J. A. Wright of Sydney joined the partners
and the firm became known as Hicks, Smith & Wright, with
an additional branch in Sydney. There was little change in the
general structure of the business until after the Second World
War, when Mr Wright retired and three separate companies
were formed as follows:

> *Hicks Smith & Sons Ltd, Wellington, New Zealand*, originally
> headed by G. Wallis-Smith (son of W. Smith) with
> branches subsequently opened in Auckland and Christ-
> church. The New Zealand manager today is Mr K. M.
> Maben.

Hicks, Smith & Sons Pty Ltd, Melbourne, Australia, originally
headed by Mr J. A. Hicks until his death in 1957 and
now managed by his son Mr W. H. Hicks.

Hicks, Smith & Sons Pty Ltd, Sydney, Australia, originally headed
by Mr W. Smith when he came over from New Zealand in
1951 to act as the Sydney manager, and on his semi-retire-
ment in 1957, replaced by Mr G. Wallis-Smith from New
Zealand. In 1960 a branch office was opened in Brisbane,
managed by Mr. B. H. Hargreaves.

In 1964 it was decided to merge the three Hicks Smith Companies with the Law Book Company of Australia and their New
Zealand subsidiary Sweet and Maxwell. A holding company
was formed to be known as the Associated Book Publishers of
Australia and New Zealand Ltd.

As might be expected, the three companies which are still
known as Hicks Smith have grown over the years and the
original staff of three has now increased to over fifty, and it is
hoped to increase it still further. Many members of the firm
have seen long service, notably Mr R. Pickering, the stationery
manager, and Mr G. B. Black, the warehouse manager, both
of whom have been with the firm for over thirty years, while
all senior staff members saw service in either the First or Second
World Wars.

The changing pattern of trade and the growth of local publishing in Australia and New Zealand have radically altered the
nature of the Hicks Smith business. In the "good old days" of
straightforward agency representation, all business was done
on indent, and the company's job was completed once it had
obtained the bookseller's order. The latter went off to London
and that, so to speak, was that.

Today, however, a continually growing number of customers
prefer to buy from locally held stocks in Australia and New
Zealand. This means in effect that the representative company
now has to have warehouse premises and staff, with sufficient
capital into the bargain to lay down the necessary stock. Hicks
Smith today, for instance, hold substantial stocks at five centres:
Brisbane, Sydney, Melbourne, Auckland and Wellington. Sometimes the management finds itself sighing for those far-off "good

old days". The aim of the new merger is to increase and divide the sales staff to give more attention to individual publishers and also to concentrate on the educational, technical, industrial and library fields.

G. E. Jubert.   France, Belgium, Holland, Scandinavia, etc.

Monsieur Jubert first heard of Warne's when an assistant in the foreign book department of a Paris bookshop before the First World War. He came to London in 1913 to work for Hachette's bookshop and was then asked to develop their export department for the sale of English books. Joining the French Army at the outbreak of war in 1914, however, he did not return to Hachette's London house until 1919. They were then situated in Chandos Street and in their export department, just a stone's throw from Warne's premises, he recalls ordering the Company's publications and receiving periodic visits from Mr Arthur King, then Warne's Export Manager.

Prior to 1939 he decided to visit Europe, and especially Scandinavia, in a free-lance capacity, to assess the market for English books and Warne's offered to let him represent them at this time. But war came in 1939, he had to rejoin the French Army and was eventually taken prisoner of war at Rouen.

Returning to London in 1947, he re-started his free-lance book representation, renewed acquaintance with Frederick Warne and became their representative for France, Holland, Belgium, Italy, Scandinavia, and latterly Spain and Portugal.

In Scandinavia M. Jubert finds a considerable interest in English books, but alas, from his point of view, a relatively small population, while in earlier days in Paris there was an English resident population and a consequent market for English books, but changing times have meant changing markets. Nevertheless, he has always found Warne's books accepted everywhere as well-produced and genuine publications, with especial reference to the Observer's series which he personally regards as a publishing miracle.

While congratulating the Company on its centenary he points out that in the same year he and his wife also celebrate their golden wedding. The Company reciprocates his good wishes.

PLATE 11

'*Mary, Mary, quite contrary*'

From *Little Folk's Book of Nursery
Rhymes*, illustrated by Rene Cloke

CHAPTER 12

Some Book Illustrators of Past and Present

During the course of the sixty years of this present century, Warne's have published many and varied illustrated books for children and a rummage among secondhand bookshelves will occasionally lead one to come across some of these earlier titles, which naturally reflect the age and period of their production. One then realizes how impossible it would often be to republish them and show such pictures to the sophisticated youngsters of these days. And yet strangely enough some of the old classical names from those days are still with us and their books still available for their devotees—Caldecott and Greenaway for instance, depicting in their drawings an even earlier day than their own and yet somehow retaining that ageless quality about their work which comes across to us over the years.

An appreciation by Anne Carroll Moore of the work of both these fine artists will be found on p. 18 of this volume. What she does not mention, however, regarding Randolph Caldecott, was the comparative shortness of his life—he was barely forty years old at his death in 1886—and by this time he had illustrated

"The Jumblies", by Edward Lear

some sixteen picture books for children as well as contributing frequently to *Punch* and *Graphic* and exhibiting occasionally at the Royal Academy in London.

Yet another artist of this period still has a small place in Warne's list today—Walter Crane—a man greatly influenced by the Arts and Crafts movement of the 1890's and one who himself was to influence others in the field of decorative book illustration. He produced a number of books on design for adult students, not under the Warne imprint, however, and in his *Decorative Illustration* of 1896 had said that "book illustration should be something more than a collection of accidental sketches. Since one cannot ignore the constructive organic element in the formation—the idea of the book itself—it is so far inartistic to leave it out of account in designing work intended to form an essential or integral part of that book." A glance at his *Baby's Opera*, for instance, which is still in Warne's Catalogue, will show how seriously he took his own advice and how each individual page takes on its own sense of design, with drawings and text fused into one.

Following on Walter Crane, one feels that people like Leslie Brooke and Beatrix Potter both sought in their own respective ways to continue this idea of a book being a unit, and as author-illustrators were able effectively to create in their minds' eye and on paper the scenes their texts were at the same time describing. Beatrix Potter was to publish her last Peter Rabbit book—*The Tale of Little Pig Robinson*—in 1930 and by this time also the art of Leslie Brooke was well known and established. Their stories are told in greater detail elsewhere in this book.

It was soon after this that Warne's were able to continue this earlier tradition with the work of another artist who saw his illustrations as an equally integral part of text and book, and the many titles which the house has published by Clifford Webb will testify to this artist-author's skill in this direction. He has for many years been famous in more adult fields as a wood-engraver of distinction, introducing colour into his designs as well as the traditional black and white, and his work for children at one time in his earlier period tended to maintain this engraved character.

One of his first books, however, *The Story of Noah*, was largely

illustrated in a formal line style, but text and pictures were both
considered as one unit on the printed page. In a later edition of
this book he was to add a coloured centre section of the animals
walking in twos towards the Ark and these coloured plates
themselves in turn also had an independent existence as a
nursery frieze, complete with a very attractive lower border of
animals, plants and insects. This lower border could not unfortunately be included in with the book illustrations.

A little later than the original *Noah*, but still of the pre-1939
era, came *Butterwick Farm* and *The North Pole Before Lunch* and
these reflected the artist's love of a wood-engraving style—
although the actual process used in the illustrations was scraperboard, then, we believe, just developing seriously as an art
technique. It is in these earlier books that one appreciates
Clifford Webb's delight in drawing animals and his pictures
have a certain friendly air about them, the farmyard animals of
Butterwick Farm for instance reminding one of the mixed farm

of tradition—sheep, cows, dogs, farmyard ducks and hens and the equally rustic farmer, his wife and the inevitable children.

His later books, beginning with *Animals from Everywhere* and continuing through to the more recent *Strange Creatures*, all equally reflect Clifford Webb's fascination for animal shape and form seen in a decorative manner; zebras, gazelles, tigers and kangaroos all being in the unmistakable stamp of the artist's style. In recent years, however, he has tended to experiment with varying techniques and appears to have developed a combined coloured crayon and "spluttered brush" style all his own. Strangely enough, his flora, as opposed to his fauna, he generally seems to consider as purely decorative and many of his flowers and plants must only grow in the artist's own private world— they are hardly of this one—and yet they can still manage to remain an essential part of the overall design.

Margaret Tarrant, another artist of an earlier epoch, and later, Molly Brett, both did some excellent work for Warne's, although in the case of each artist the main bulk of their work lay in other directions than ours. Margaret Tarrant's work was always of a traditional water-colour style with an obvious appreciation and love of children, while Molly Brett's work in the realm of nursery pictures, full of rabbits and elves, mice and birds, must have brought delight to many a child and livened up many a classroom wall.

Somewhat slightly different in style, but with the same sense of fun and charm when drawing animals, is the more recent work of Patricia Turner, with her illustrations for the "Tim" books of Ella Monckton. Miss Turner works almost "same size" —which means that she draws her illustrations just a shade larger than they finally appear in the book and the painstaking care she puts into each whisker of Tim is only matched by the fascinating detail she manages to cram into the interior of Tim's father's general village store, with its pans and tins and bags of sugar and heaven knows what.

On a completely different note from the above artist is the work of an author-artist whose books Warne's have been producing steadily over the past few years. She is Inga Borg, of Sweden, who has a very distinctive style of her own. Miss Borg's books are published simultaneously in her native Swedish and

From "Strange Creatures" by Clifford Webb

in English, but although the language may change, the pictures very fortunately do not and for British readers particularly there must be that added sense of another and more Northern atmosphere. This is marked in her illustrations for such books as *Parrak the White Reindeer*, *Tramper the Elk* and *Bru the Brown Bear*. Inga Borg's style is direct and forceful with a fine sense of colour and mood, while the strength of her brush strokes suggests her complete confidence both in her medium of water-colour and her ability to render the effect she is striving for. Many of her pictures can be recalled afterwards, so vivid at times can be their initial impact.

Hubert Williams is yet another artist whose work has impressed itself with Warne's over recent years. Mr Williams, besides his work as an illustrator, also works privately as a portrait painter and flower artist. His lively sense of colour, and the general air of freshness to his illustrations, coupled with the look of all his children being "well brought up" and his adults being pleasant neighbourly people, make his drawings of particular value when considering the educational side of a book's life. We understand that he gets many of his models, particularly of children, from among the local "small fry" and one gets the impression that they must be a very pleasant lot down on the Hertfordshire–Essex border where he lives.

In contrast to the varying styles previously referred to is the work of Miss K. Nixon, a fine animal artist who has treated her subject seriously in such books as *Animal Mothers and Babies* and *Bird Families* and again in a slightly more humorous vein in books dealing with her characters Pushti and Poo. These latter two are both pets of the artist—Pushti being a Siamese kitten and Poo a favourite dachshund—and her skill lies in rendering their two distinct personalities against strong colourful backgrounds, particularly of flowers and foliage. Miss Nixon once spent a considerable time abroad, painting scenes of animals, birds and flowers with a striking sense of colour and pattern which evoked far warmer and sunnier skies than our own. The writer can recall seeing an exhibition of her work, held here in a gallery in London's Bond Street, following her eventual return home. It was soon after this period that she began publishing her work with Warne's.

From "Tim Minds the Shop",
drawing by Patricia W. Turner

In the realm of fairy story and nursery rhyme the House has been fortunate in obtaining the services of Rene Cloke for its Little Folks series and here her bright cheerful colouring, her ability to give her mice, pigs and roosters an almost human expression, but devoid of mere caricature, have caused her work to be much admired by all of us here. Her love of small detail too—the odd butterfly or toadstool—add those extra touches of interest which can help to develop that sense of observation among small children and rouse their interest in discovering yet something else in a nursery rhyme picture. Miss Cloke's drawings of children, whether of their being good or up to mischief, can be equally as attractive as her animal sketches and as sympathetically rendered.

One has no wish to compile a mere catalogue and of necessity many names must be left out of a short review of the firm's output on the general illustration side over the years. One might in passing, however, recall the work of H. M. Brock, who did so much good sound work in earlier days for many publishers and illustrated a fine *Book of Nursery Tales* for Warne's which still has its place in the list. The work of Lawson Wood may also be recalled, with his *Mr* and *Mrs* books no doubt selling in their

From "*The Book of Nursery Tales*",
drawing by *H. M. Brock*

thousands in their day, and his name being one among many artists who served the firm in their time.

Equally also one can recall during the 1920's and 1930's all the dozens of adventure and school stories for the children of both sexes, for whom such fare must have been a major imaginative outlet in those far-off days before television and the picture-strip type of publication made their influence felt so strongly. Artists such as Reginald Mills, T. Cuneo and D. C. Eyles come to mind, among many, as illustrators of these books in which manly youths fought foreign bandits and girls fresh from high-school sailed with Daddy to India and adventure. All these stories—the natural continuation of those of Henty and the *Boys Own Paper*—are now as far removed from the life of today as are the wars of Troy. Their very general name in the book trade as Reward books has something of an old ring about it too, reminding one of the days when to be given a book of this type as a prize was an event in life. Such books might be read and re-read by their lucky owners until whole paragraphs could be memorized by mere repetition.

Today, modern printing methods, particularly in the field of offset lithography, have greatly added to the colour, gaiety and variety of the children's book. Type design and layout, too, play their part, and the amount of thought and genuine care which may often go into the making of a successful children's book sometimes, one feels, should almost be blazoned on the cover.

The children of today are in that sense lucky by the sheer range in topic, size and price of the books which publishers produce for their special needs and it can be safely said that the illustrations are invariably given careful consideration.

We here at Warne's, conscious both of our old tradition and of our vital need to keep abreast of the times, do what we can in our own way to keep the flag flying. Let us hope we may so continue into our second century, even if a Kate Greenaway or a Beatrix Potter are only born once in a lifetime.

From "Complete Version of Ye Three Blind Mice",
drawing by Walton Corbould